JOHN BASKERVILLE

TYPE-FOUNDER

AND PRINTER

1706-1775

BY

Josiah Henry Benton, LL.D.

BOSTON

PRIVATELY PRINTED

1914

NOTE

I have, for some years, been interested in John Baskerville, and have collected his imprints. Knowing this fact, the President of the Boston Society of Printers asked me to prepare a paper on Baskerville, to be read at a meeting of the Society on February 24, 1914. This I did, and that paper formed the basis of this little book.

J. H. B.

JOHN BASKERVILLE

JOHN BASKERVILLE, a great English type-founder and printer, was born in January, 1706, and died in January, 1775, having lived nearly the full period of threescore years and ten. To understand him and what he did, we must know something of the time and place in which he lived. It was a time when the great middle classes of England were coming into power. The divine right of kings was destroyed at Culloden in 1745. England was slowly awakening from the deadly languor of the corruption of Walpole's government. Whitefield was preaching, and Wesley was preaching and organizing. The middle classes grew stronger every day and kept Pitt, with his intense patriotism and extravagance, in power, in spite of the upper classes. The rule of England in the East began in 1757, when Clive, on June 23, fought the battle of Plassey. Frederick the Great, aided by the liberal subsidies of Pitt, fought the battle of Rossbach in November, 1757, and the battle of Minden in November, 1759, thus laying the foundation of the German Empire which has always been at peace with England. The capture of Montreal in 1760 established the English ascendancy in the New World. During this period the English Empire came into being because of the rule of the commercial middle class.

Birmingham was even then a great middle-class town; a place of about 30,000 inhabitants, noted for its varied manufactures, but more noted for its freedom, by which it seemed to have the power of attracting within its boundaries artisans of every trade and every degree of skill. It accorded almost perfect freedom to all. Dissenters, Baptists, Methodists, Roman Catholics, Jews, Quakers, and heretics of all sorts were welcomed, and were undisturbed in their religious observances. No trades unions, no trade guilds, no companies existed. The system of apprentices was only partially known. Every man was free to come and go, to found, or to follow, or to leave a trade, just as he chose. Birmingham was emphatically the town of free trade, where no restrictions, commercial or municipal, existed.

Into this community young Baskerville came. It was particularly suited to him. He was a free thinker. He was active, industrious, inventive, persistent. He thought out and did new things.*

His first occupation, when he was seventeen years old, was that of a servant in the house of a clergyman, who discovered that Baskerville was skilled in penmanship and set him to teaching the poor boys in the parish the art of writing.

The post of writing-master at King Edward's School in Birmingham fell vacant, and Baskerville took it and taught writing and bookkeeping there. In the mean time he had become very much interested in calligraphy, and turned his skill in writing to the cutting of stones. Of his actual stone-cutting work only two specimens have been preserved, the most important of which is in the churchyard at Edgbaston. There is also a small square slate slab with the inscription: "Grave Stones Cut in any of the Hands by John Baskervill Writing Master." It is to be noted that the final e was not added to Baskerville's name until after he became more prosperous. In the fine lettering of this inscription it is easy to trace the foundation of those forms of type which Baskerville afterwards used in printing. He practised writing during the years 1733, 1734, and 1735, being rated for school taxes at a sixpence.

* *Birmingham and the Midland Hardware District, pages 211, 221.*

About the year 1736 one John Taylor came to Birmingham and introduced japanned ware in the shape of indoor utensils and articles of personal or other ornament. From the smallest beginnings Taylor created a business out of which he had acquired a fortune of £200,000 when he died at the age of fifty-four. To Taylor we owe the gilt button and gilt snuff-box, the painted snuff-box, and the numerous race of enamels.

Baskerville had a great desire to obtain money, and as he was a good draughtsman and had a turn for painting, it occurred to him that the best thing he could do would be to produce goods painted and japanned as they never had been painted and japanned before. He dropped his writing-materials and set himself to learn the secrets of japanning. It is said that he obtained his knowledge of Mr. Taylor's cheap and excellent varnish for snuff-boxes, which was a secret, by following him to every place and shop where he went and ordering precisely the same species, kind, and quality of articles that he had ordered. He thus learned not only the ingredients of the varnish, but their proportions.

Baskerville had that which is rare, — business capacity in connection with artistic taste, — and he soon built up a flourishing business. In 1749 he carried on a great trade in the japan art, making such useful things as candlesticks, stands, salvers, waiters, bread-trays, tea-boards, etc., which were elegantly designed and highly finished. His ingenuity continually suggested improvements both in the materials of which he made use and in the methods adopted in the manufacture, while he had a genius in selecting as workmen those who were best fitted for their occupation. One of his advertisements reads as follows: "Any boy of a decent Family who has a Genius and Turn for Drawing will be taken on trial on moderate terms. Any Painters of tolerable Abilities may have constant employment."

In 1742 he obtained a patent for "a new method of making and flat grinding thin metal plates and of working or fashioning the same by means of iron rolls and swages." The plates were japanned and varnished to "produce fine glowing Mohogony Colour and Black no way inferior to the most perfect India goods, or an imitation of Tortoise shell which greatly excels Nature, both in Colour and Hardness." It will be seen that this patent embodied to a great extent the same principle that Baskerville employed in his later treatment of paper. In the japan business Baskerville competed with Taylor, not so much in making the things Taylor made as in making better ones and different ones. A curious thing about Baskerville's japan work is that no authentic specimen has come down to us.

In a few years he amassed a considerable fortune in that business. He took a building lease of eight acres in the northeast part of Birmingham, to which he gave the name of *Easy Hill*, and there he built a house at an expense of about £6000, or $30,000, equivalent to at least $60,000 to-day. This place is described by Alexander Carlyle as follows: "Baskerville's house was a quarter of a mile from the town, and in its way handsome and elegant. What struck us most was his first kitchen, which was most completely furnished with everything that could be wanted, kept as clean and bright as if it had come straight from the shop, for it was used, and the fineness of the kitchen was a great point in the family, for here they received their company, and there we were entertained with coffee and chocolate."* Derrick, in a letter written to the Earl of Cork, July 15, 1760, says: "I need not remind your Lordship, that Baskerville, one of the best printers in the world, was born in this town, and resides near it. His house stands at about half a mile distance, on an eminence that commands a fine prospect. I paid him a visit, and was received with great politeness, though an entire stranger. His apartments are elegant; his stair-case is particularly curious; and the room in which he dines, and calls a smoking-room is very handsome. The grate and furniture belonging to it are, I think, of bright wrought iron, and cost him a round sum. He has just completed an elegant octavo Common Prayer Book, has a scheme for publishing a grand folio edition of the Bible; and will soon finish a beautiful collection of Fables, by the ingenious Mr. Dodsley. He manufactures his own paper, types, and ink; and they are remarkably good. This ingenious artist carries on a great trade in the japan way, in which he shewed me several useful articles, such as candlesticks, stands, salvers, waiters, bread-baskets, tea-boards, &c. elegantly designed and highly finished. Baskerville is a great cherisher of genius, which, wherever he finds it, he loses no opportunity of cultivating. One of his workmen has manifested fine talents for fruit painting in several pieces which he shewed me."

A writer in the Birmingham "Daily Mail" of February 3, 1886, thus describes the Easy Hill residence: "The pasture was luxuriant, great elm trees shaded the parklike expanse of verdure, an ample fish-pond stretched away westwards, and a picturesque disused windmill standing upon a slight elevation was ready to be converted into the most captivating of summer houses. . . . Of the house which he built for himself we have engravings, and

* *Autobiography of Alexander Carlyle, D.D.*

as many remains as one would care to preserve of that particular style of architecture."

Hutton, the historian of Birmingham, says Baskerville previously lived at No. 22 in Moor-street, and that having obtained a building lease, "two furlongs north of the town, he converted it into a little Eden, and built a houſe in the center; but the town, as if conſcious of his merit, followed his retreat, and ſurrounded it with buildings. . . . Here he continued the buſineſs of a japanner for life: his carriage, each pannel of which was a diſtinſt picture, might be conſidered the *pattern-card of his trade*, and was drawn by a beautiful pair of cream-coloured horſes." This chariot was one of the wonders of Birmingham, one section richly gilt and painted with little naked cupids and flowers, drawn by two cream-colored horses with net hangings almost to the ground. The panels were said to be each in the nature of a picture, got up Japan-wise.* He became High Bailiff of Birmingham in 1761. His duties were to inſpect the market and rectify weights and dry measures; also to make proclamation of two fairs each year; and to give a dinner to the other municipal officers, at which it is said that an expense of £40 was incurred. This dinner was intended for business, but, in the quaint language of the historian of the time, "It was too early to begin business till the table was well stored with bottles, and too late afterwards." He affected clothes of the most gorgeous description. His favorite dress was said to have been green, edged with a narrow gold lace, a scarlet waistcoat with a very broad gold lace, and a small round hat likewise edged with lace. It is said that he attended a funeral in a new suit of bright colors and gold lace.

All this show created a suspicion in the public mind that

* *Hutton's History of Birmingham (1783), page 90.*

Baskerville was in financial trouble, so that at one time he published a refutation of some charges of that kind in the Birmingham "Gazette." He sought to find the author of the charges, declaring that "Whoever can discover the author, or give a clue by which he may be traced, will by informing me lay me under the highest obligations of gratitude."

In these letters he said that he had "often wished an additional Article in the Litany for the Use of Tradesmen, — From Bad Debts and Bankrupts, Good Lord deliver us."

A Mrs. Eaves went to live at Easy Hill about 1750. She took her two daughters, and very likely her son, with her. She had made an unfortunate marriage with one Richard Eaves, who, "having been found guilty of some fraudulent practices in regard to a relation's will, was obliged to quit the kingdom." * Her husband left her without money or any means of support. Baskerville became interested in her, and she went to his house probably as a housekeeper. Shortly afterwards Baskerville and she were living together as man and wife. Although her husband was not known to be dead, she passed as Mrs. Baskerville. She accompanied him to London to visit Dodsley, and was everywhere received as his wife. It does not appear that his social position in Birmingham was at all impaired by this connection. He was very kind and attentive to Mrs. Eaves, and when Eaves died, Baskerville married the widow in June, 1764. They had one son, who died in infancy. Baskerville was inconsolable, and in a letter to Franklin gave the death of his son as one of the reasons for desiring to sell his type in France. He said: "Let the reason of my parting with it be the death of my son and intended successor."

When Baskerville began the work that made him famous, he

* *Gough's British Topography (1780), volume ii, page 306.*

was a middle-aged man, fifty years old, who had amassed a large fortune, and was living in quiet comfort on his own estate. He was carrying on a very large and lucrative japanning business, which he continued to conduct during his life. He was a person of much consequence in Birmingham when he took up the matter of type-founding and printing.

As for Baskerville's private character, we have the accounts of his friends and of his critics, and it is not easy to come to a just conclusion. Hutton, in his "History of Birmingham,"* says: "In private life he was a humorift; idle† in the extreme; but his invention was of the true Birmingham model, active. He could well defign, but procured others to execute; wherever he found merit he careffed it: he was remarkably polite to the ftranger; fond of fhew: a figure rather of the fmaller fize, and delighted to adorn that figure with gold lace. . . . Although conftructed with the light timbers of a frigate, his movement was folemn as a fhip of the line. During the twenty-five years I knew him, though in the decline of life, he retained the fingular traces of a handfome man. If he exhibited a peevifh‡ temper, we may confider good nature and intenfe thinking are not always found together. Tafte accompanied him through the different walks of agriculture, architecture, and the finer arts. Whatever paffed through his fingers, bore the lively marks of John Bafkerville."

Chambers, in his "Biographical Illustrations of Worcestershire," gives an interesting sketch of Baskerville, in which his will is printed with the exception of those portions where, as, Mr. Chambers regrets to say, Baskerville "unblushingly avows

* *Hutton's History of Birmingham, page 90.*
† *Frivolous.*　　‡ *Testy.*

not only his disbelief of, but his contempt for revealed religion, and that in terms too gross for repetition." Chambers was evidently not a partial critic. He records the fact that Mr. Noble,* who well remembered Baskerville, says he taught his respected father to write, and he maintained an acquaintance with him as long as he lived. "I have been very often with him to Baskerville's house, and found him ever a most profane wretch, and ignorant of literature to a wonderful degree. I have seen many of his letters, which, like his will, were not written grammatically; nor could he even spell well. In person, he was a shrivelled old coxcomb. His favourite dress was green, edged with a narrow gold lace, a scarlet waistcoat, with a very broad gold lace; and a small round hat, likewise edged with gold lace. His wife was all that affectation can describe: she lived with him in adultery many years. She was originally a servant: such a pair are rarely met with. He had wit; but it was always at the expense of religion and decency, particularly if in company with the clergy. I have often thought there was much similarity in his person to Voltaire, whose sentiments he was ever retailing."

Mr. Paterson, in a letter in Nichols's "Literary Anecdotes," wrote: "I could give you also a note on Baskerville, to demonstrate that he knew very little of the execution of typography

---

* *Mark Noble, who was born in Birmingham in 1754. His father sold beads, knives, toys, etc., to the slave traders. In 1781 he was presented to two "starvation livings," as he called them, in Warwickshire. He divided his interests then among his congregation, his books, and his farm. His writings were those of an imperfectly educated, vulgar-minded man. His ignorance of English grammar and composition rendered his books hard to read and occasionally unintelligible, while the moral reflections with which they abounded were puerile. (Dictionary of National Biography.)*

beyond the common productions which are to be found every day in Paternoster-row, and therefore, in a comparative view, might readily conclude that he had outstript them all." But, adds Chambers, "Dibdin, whose judgment in these matters few will call in question, says that 'Rowe Mores, in his abuse of Baskerville, exhibits the painful and perhaps mirth-provoking efforts of a man kicking against the thorns. Baskerville was a wonderful creature ɔ an artist, but a vain and silly man.'"

Many lies were told about Baskerville and his work.

The following from the "European Magazine" (December, 1785, page 463) is a fair sample. A correspondent, whose name is not disclosed, but who signs himself *Viator*, makes the following statement, to which Mr. Chambers gives place in his "Biographical Illustrations of Worcestershire:" "I was acquainted with Baskerville, the printer, but cannot wholly agree with the extracts concerning him, from Hutton's History of Birmingham. It is true he was very ingenious in mechanics, but it is also well known he was extremely illiterate, and his jokes and sarcasms on the Bible, with which his conversation abounded, shewed the most contemptible ignorance of eastern history and manners, and indeed of every thing. His quarto edition of Milton's Paradise Lost, with all its splendour, is a deep disgrace to the English press. He could not spell himself, and knew not who could. A Warwickshire country schoolmaster, of some parish charity school, we presume, was employed by him to correct this splendid edition, and that dunce has spelt many words in it according to the vulgar Warwickshire pronunciation. For example, many of the western vulgar clap an *h* to every word beginning with an open vowel, or even the *w*, as *hood* for *wood*, my *harm* for my *arm*, *heggs* for *eggs*, &c., &c., and again as viciously drop-

Dear Sr.   Birmm. 20 Decr. 1756

I have for some part hoped a line from you in relation to
the paper Scheme; Whether you have sent, or chose to send any
of the thin post to Mr. Calver, as that is the only Article I lay
any stress upon in his hands; pray do not send it if you are more
inclined to keep it; He shall stay till I can furnish him, which
probably may bee six Weeks or two months; I have not more than
six ream of that sort, which if I chose to do it, I would sell tomorrow
in Birmm. at 24s. & if inserting his names makes the least difference
in yr. Scheme of Advertising, I shall like it quite as well left
out. I have sent Samples of the ornamented paper & thin post
gilt to several neighbouring towns & have received Orders freely from
them; I told you in my last the prices, but that need not bee a Rule
to you, perhaps some of yr. Customers would like them less if sold
too low all I feared was laying an Embargo on them. I propose
reducing the Price of the octavo from 21 to 18 as it will be
more suitable to the Quarto. pray therefore make me Dr. for that
Difference in all yr. Stock of that sort. Pray give me yr. opinion
if it would bee wrong to make a present of a quire of each sort &
the thin gilt, to the Prince of Wales, as a Sample of English
manufactory, to be had at Mr. Dodsley's; the Present mine?

I copied with great pleasure from our Birm. Paper a long
Complemt. made you, which I shall learn by heart, & of which I
give you Joy. I shall have Virgil out of the Press by the latter
End of Jany. & hope to produce the Volumes as smooth as the best
Paper I have sent you. Pray will it not bee proper to advertise
how near it is finishing, & beg the Gentlemen who intend fa-
vouring me with their Names to send them by that time.

When this is done, I can print nothing at home but another
Classick (a Specimen of which will be given with it) which I

cannot forbear thinking a grievous hardships, after the infinite pains & great expence I have been at. I have almost a mind to print a pocket Classicks in one size larger than the old Elzivers as the difference will on comparison be obvious. to every Scholer nor should I be very sollicitous whether it paid me or not.

You have not fulfilled y.r promise in sending me the print c.s Scheme. I am with due Respect to M.r James Dodsley & Comp.t of the ensuing Season———

D.r S.r

Y.r obed.t Serv.t

J. Baskerville

ping the *h* in verbs, as *ave* for *have*, *as* for *has*, &c., &c. Many
instances of this horrid ignorance we find in the ingenious Baskerville's splendid Milton, where *as* is often put for the verb *has*,
and *has* for the conjunction *as*, with several others of this worse
than *cockney* family. Nor can I by any means agree with Mr.
Hutton that 'it is to the lasting discredit of the British nation
that no purchaser could be found for his types.'—What was the
merit of his printing?—His paper was of a finer gloss, and his
ink of a brighter black than ordinary; his type was thicker than
usual in the thick strokes, and finer in the fine, and was sharp-
ened at the angles in a novel manner; all these combined gave
his editions a brilliant rich look, when his pages were turned
lightly over; but when you sit down to read them, the eye is
almost immediately fatigued with the gloss of the paper and
ink, and the sharp angles of the type; and it is universally known
that Baskerville's printing is *not* read; that the better sort of
the London printing is infinitely preferable for use, and even for
real sterling elegance. The Universities and London booksellers
therefore are not to be blamed for declining the purchase of Baskerville's types, which we are told were bought by a Society at
Paris, where tawdry silk and tinsel is preferred to the finest English broad cloth, or even Genoa velvet." *

This spiteful story has thus been in type and reproduced in
one form and another for more than a hundred years. Nobody
appears to have questioned it, and yet it is false, and maliciously
so. An examination of the quarto edition of Milton's "Paradise
Lost" shows that "as" is never put for the verb "has," and "has"
is never put for the conjunction "as." There is no such word in the
book as "eggs," and no such combination of words as "my arm."

Chambers's Biographical Illustrations.

It is impossible to find there the mistakes which *Viator* says are in this book and make it "a deep disgrace to the English press."

For some reason, probably because he did better work than other printers, and produced books without so much regard to profit as they were obliged to consider, Baskerville's work was very much criticised by other printers in his time. Dr. Bedford said: " By Baskerville's specimen of his types you will perceive how much the elegance of them is owing to the paper, which he makes himself as well as the types and the ink also; I was informed that whenever they come to be used by common pressmen and common materials they lose their beauty considerably." It is now certain that he did not make his paper. Certainly he made it for no books except Virgil and the Milton. Rowe Mores,* in "English Typographical Founders and Founderies," 1778 (page 86), said: " Mr. Baskerville of Birmingham, that enterprizing place, made some attempts at letter-cutting, but desisted and with good reason. The Greek cut by him, or his, for the University of Oxford is execrable. Indeed, he can hardly claim a place amongst letter-cutters. His typographical excellence lay more in his trim, glossy paper to dim the sight." In a note upon this passage John Nichols said: "The idea entertained by Mr. Mores of the ingenious Mr. Baskerville is certainly a just one. His glossy paper and too sharp type offend the patience of a reader more sensibly than the innovations I have already censured."

---

* *Edward Rowe Mores was a crusty, crabbed clergyman, who collected different founts of types, and obtained much information upon the subject of type-founding. He printed eighty copies of the book quoted above, and Nichols bought the whole of them. See Nichols's Literary Anecdotes, volume v, page 389.*

Nichols was a rival printer. He was apprenticed to William Bowyer, of whom he was an executor and the residuary legatee. All his prejudices were against Baskerville and his work. He wrote many books, but they were mostly by hirelings, the blunders only being his own. He reached the summit of his ambition when he became Master of the Stationers' Company in 1804.

The following letter from Franklin explains the prejudice and ignorance with respect to Baskerville's work: " Let me give you a pleasant instance of the prejudice some have entertained against your work. Soon after I returned, discoursing with a gentleman concerning the artists of Birmingham, he said you would be the means of blinding all the readers of the nation, for the strokes of your letters being too thin and narrow, hurt the eye, and he could never read a line of them without pain. 'I thought,' said I, 'you were going to complain of the gloss on the paper some object to.' 'No, no,' said he, ' I have heard that mentioned, but it is not that; it is in the form and cut of the letters themselves, they have not that height and thickness of the stroke which makes the common printing so much more comfortable to the eye.' You see this gentleman was a connoisseur. In vain I endeavoured to support your character against the charge; he knew what he felt, and could see the reason of it, and several other gentlemen among his friends had made the same observation, etc. Yesterday he called to visit me, when, mischievously bent to try his judgement, I stepped into my closet, tore off the top of Mr. Caslon's Specimen, and produced it to him as yours, brought with me from Birmingham saying, I had been examining it, since he spoke to me, and could not for my life perceive the disproportion he mentioned, desiring him to point it out to me. He readily undertook it, and went over the several founts, showing me everywhere what he thought instances of that disproportion; and declared that he could not then read the specimen without feeling very strongly the pain he had mentioned to me. I spared him that time the confusion of being told, that these were the types he had been reading all his life, with so much ease to his eyes; the types his adored Newton is printed with, on which he has pored not a little; nay the very types his own book is printed with (for he himself is an author), and yet never discovered the painful disproportion in them, till he thought they were yours."

Burton says: "A collector, with a taste for the inaccurate, might easily satiate it in the editions, so attractive in their deceptive beauty, of the great Birmingham printer, Baskerville."* Reed says: "Despite the splendid appearance of his impressions, the ordinary English printers viewed with something like suspicion the meretricious combination of sharp type and hot-pressed paper which lent to his sheets their extraordinary brilliancy. They objected to the dazzling effect thus produced on the eye; they found fault with the unevenness of tone and colour in different parts of the same book, and even discovered an irregularity and lack of symmetry in some of his types, which his glossy paper and bright ink alike failed to disguise."†

Both these statements are obviously untrue. An examination of Baskerville's books shows that they are accurate, or at least the inaccuracies are only those of the editions from which they are reprinted, and the combination of paper, ink, and type is necessary to make a really fine book.

"In private life," Reed remarks, "he was a bundle of para-

* *The Bookhunter (1885), page 67.*
† *Reed's Old English Letter Foundries, pages 269, 271, 277, 279.*

doxes. He was an exemplary son, and an affectionate, judicious husband, but full of personal animosities. . . . In person he was a shrivelled old coxcomb, but in spirit he was a worker of unquenchable energy. Peevish in temper, he was a charming host. . . . The one thing that reconciled all was his strong personality. Whatever else he was he was never commonplace."

"He was one of those men," says a writer in the "Secular Review," "who strove for excellence, and was not satisfied until he obtained it. Whatever he undertook to do he not only did well, but better than his predecessors, and he was in truth a genuine national reformer." The editor of the "Beauties of Worcestershire" calls Baskerville "a most useful and *estimable character*," and says he was of an "ancient family, as old as the Conquest." This may be taken with some salt. Perhaps the best evidence of the sort of man he was is found in the impression that he made upon the most eminent men of his time, by the thoroughness and energy of his life, his originality of taste, his fine pride in perfect work, his stoutness of courage, and his honorable impartiality in printing works with which he coincided, and those which represented the religious views of his countrymen from which he himself dissented.*

Dr. Carlyle thus speaks of a visit to him: "We passed the day in seeing the Baskerville press, and Baskerville himself, who was a great curiosity. . . . Baskerville was on hand with his folio Bible at this time, and Garbett insisted on being allowed to subscribe for Home and Robertson. Home's absence afflicted him, for he had seen and heard of the tragedy of *Douglas*. Robertson hitherto had no name, and the printer said bluntly that he would rather have one subscription to his work of a man like Mr. Home,

* *Dent and Straus, John Baskerville, page 64.*

than an hundred ordinary men. He dined with us that day, and acquitted himself so well that Robertson pronounced him a man of genius, while James Adam and I thought him but a prating pedant."* Kippis adds "his own testimony concerning Mr. Baskerville's politeness to strangers, and the cheerful hospitality with which he treated those who were introduced to him. He was well known to many ingenious men."

Baskerville belonged to the literary club in Birmingham, called the "Luna Club," which used to meet on the nights of the full moon, so that the members might have a light to go home by. Hence the name of the members — "the Lunaticks." It had among its members many most famous men. Wedgwood, the potter; Dr. Erasmus Darwin, the poet; Thomas Day, author of "Sanford and Merton;" Sir William Herschel, the astronomer; Sir Joseph Banks, the naturalist; Samuel Galton; Dr. Withering, the botanist and physician to the General Hospital at Birmingham; and others of like character were all members of it.

Baskerville had his own taste about the printing and decoration of his books. When Dodsley sent a plate to him to be included in a volume he was printing, Baskerville told him that his own taste would not permit him to use the plate. He said: "If you will accept my judgment and skill, it is at your service."† In fact, Baskerville always had his own way, and did things as he wished to do them, and whatever credit there is for his productions is due to him alone. Tedder says that "his social virtues were considerable — a good son, an affectionate father and kinsman, polite and hospitable to strangers — he was entirely without the jealousy commonly ascribed to the artist

Autobiography of Alexander Carlyle, D.D.

†*Straus, Robert Dodsley, page 272.*

and inventor. Birmingham has contributed many distinguished men to the industrial armies of England; but there are few of whom she has more reason to be proud than the skilful genius who was at once the British Aldus Manutius and the finest printer of modern times." *

He was very intimate with Dodsley, the bookseller, a man of great property and of irreproachable character, who stayed with him when in Birmingham, and with whom Baskerville stayed when he was in London. † His correspondence with Shenstone is quite voluminous, and with Benjamin Franklin he had very excellent relations. Franklin visited him in Birmingham, advised him in his printing affairs, and in the proposed sale of his type when he was about to give up business. It is not likely, if he had been profane and ignorant, that he would have remained on such terms with such people. The trouble seems to have been that he refused to put himself on a par with other printers, and insisted that he did much better work than anybody else; this of course brought the whole clamjamfrie down on him.

Baskerville had probably very little taste for letters as such. He printed the books which, in the estimation of the public, were most important. He was a type-founder and printer, not a scholar. He printed Bibles and Prayer Books not because he believed in Christianity, but because they were the books which everybody used and which he thought warranted the most effective treatment. I think he can hardly be said to have printed a book which represented his ideas, unless it be Shaftesbury's "Characteristicks," which was brought out in 1773, and is a beautiful specimen of his printing. He admired the satire of "Hudi-

* *Dictionary of National Biography.*

† *Straus, Robert Dodsley, pages 219, 273.*

bras" and was fond of quoting it, and as Shenstone says, "was seized with a violent inclination to publish 'Hudibras,' his favorite poem, in a pompous quarto in an entire new set of cuts." He liked Voltaire, and is said to have quoted him constantly. He sent copies of the editions of Virgil and Milton to Voltaire at Ferney, and proposed to him to print some work of his. Voltaire replied in English, "I thank you earnestly for the honour you do me. I send you an exemplary by the way of Holland." Baskerville set up some sheets from the copy which was sent him and returned them to Voltaire, who replied, "The old scribbler to whom you have been so kind as to send your magnificent editions of Virgil and Milton thanks you heartily. He will send you as soon as possible his poor sheets duly corrected. They stand in great need of it." * Beyond this fondness for "Hudibras" and admiration for Voltaire, we have nothing to show that Baskerville cared anything for letters. He was artistic, but at the same time mercenary and vain. He meant to print books such as had never been printed, and he expected that people would buy them and pay the expense. When they did not, he became disgusted and gave up the work for two or three years. Then, spurred into action by the attempt of Boden, a rival printer in Birmingham, to print a Bible, he came again into the field and printed some of his finest works. But all the time he was in bad temper because his books cost him so much money and he got so little back. He wrote Walpole that he should be obliged to sell his little patrimony, that he had borrowed £2000 to print the Cambridge Bible. He continually looked out for little expenses. In a letter to Dodsley he says, "As you are in the Land of Franks, half a Doz would do me a peculiar pleasure, as a good many things

* *Lettres inédites de Voltaire (1857), page 254.*

not worth a Groat might be communicated by, &c." He was excessively self-confident. He considered himself different from others. He thought that whatever was brought into being by Baskerville was therefore a fine thing, and truth compels us to say he was probably right. His japan work was better than that of any one else, and his printing was the finest that England had seen or has since seen.

So much for Baskerville the man. We have now to see what he did as a type-founder and printer.

At the beginning of the century there was no real type foundry in England. Nearly all the type used was imported from Holland, but in 1737 Samuel Caslon, who was a gunsmith's apprentice, issued a specimen sheet of his founts of type, and after that England could depend upon her own resources for types. William Caslon, brother to Samuel, afterward lived with a Birmingham type-maker named William Anderton, who printed a little specimen of Great Primer, Roman and Italic. Baskerville probably became acquainted with Anderton. At any rate, there is here an explanation of the way in which the japanner's interest became aroused in the designing and making of founts of type for purposes of printing. Much of the beauty of type depends upon the printer, and therefore Baskerville soon came to see that he must print with the types which he cut. From the very commencement of his experiments in type-founding he was determined to occupy himself both with type-founding and printing. It also occurred to him to introduce a new kind of paper which had been finished in a certain way. In a word, he wished to use processes for books very similar to those which he had used for his japanned goods. His proposals, therefore, took the following shape. There was to be a new typography, and for its introduction four points were to be considered: First, the character of the types themselves; secondly, the press; thirdly, the paper and ink; and lastly, the actual mode of printing.

It is fortunate that in the preface to the second book which Baskerville printed — Milton's "Paradise Lost" — he took the world into his confidence. It is the only preface written by him. He said: "Amongst the feveral mechanic Arts that have engaged my attention, there is no one which I have purfued with fo much fteadinefs and pleafure, as that of *Letter-Founding*. Having been an early admirer of the beauty of Letters, I became infenfibly defirous of contributing to the perfection of them. I formed to my felf Ideas of greater accuracy than had yet appeared, and have endeavoured to produce a *Sett* of *Types* according to what I conceived to be their true proportion.

"*Mr. Caflon* is an Artift, to whom the Republic of Learning has great obligations; his ingenuity has left a fairer copy for my emulation, than any other mafter. In his great variety of *Characters* I intend not to follow him; the *Roman* and *Italic* are all I have hitherto attempted; if in thefe he has left room for improvement, it is probably more owing to that variety which divided his attention, than to any other caufe. I honor his merit, and only wifh to derive fome fmall fhare of Reputation, from an Art which proves accidentally to have been the object of our mutual purfuit.

"After having fpent many years, and not a little of my fortune in my endeavours to advance this art; I muft own it gives me great Satisfaction, to find that my Edition of *Virgil* has been fo favorably received. The improvement in the Manufacture of the *Paper*, the *Colour*, and *Firmnefs* of the *Ink* were not overlooked; nor did the accuracy of the workmanſhip in general, paſs unregarded. If the judicious found ſome imperfections in the *firſt attempt*, I hope the preſent work will ſhew that a proper uſe has been made of their Criticiſms: I am conſcious of this at leaſt, that I received them as I ever ſhall, with that degree of deference which every private man owes to the Opinion of the public.

"It is not my deſire to print many books; but ſuch only, as are *books* of *Conſequence*, of *intrinſic merit*, or *eſtablished Reputation*, and which the public may be pleaſed to ſee in an elegant dreſs, and to purchaſe at ſuch a price, as will repay the extraordinary care and expence that muſt neceſſarily be beſtowed upon them. Hence I was deſirous of making an experiment upon ſome one of our beſt Engliſh Authors, among thoſe *Milton* appeared the moſt eligible. And I embrace with pleaſure the opportunity of acknowledging in this public manner the generoſity of *Mr. Tonſon;* who with ſingular politeneſs complimented me with the privilege of printing an entire Edition of that *Writers Poetical Works.*

"In the execution of this deſign, if I have followed with exactneſs the Text of *Dr. Newton,* it is all the merit of *that kind* which I pretend to claim. But if this performance ſhall appear to perſons of judgment and penetration, in the *Paper, Letter, Ink* and *Workmanſhip* to excel; I hope their approbation may contribute to procure for me what would indeed be the extent of my Ambition, a power to print an Octavo *Common-Prayer Book,* and a Folio Bible.

"Should it be my good fortune to meet with this indulgence, I wou'd uſe my utmoſt efforts to perfect an Edition of them with the greateſt Elegance and Correctneſs; a work which I hope might do some honor to the Englifh Prefs, and contribute to improve the pleafure, which men of true tafte will always have in the perufal of thofe *facred Volumes.*"

This preface shows clearly the purpose with which Basker-ville entered upon type-founding and printing. He desired to ad-vance this art, not by printing many books, but only books of consequence or established reputation, which the public would be pleased to see in an elegant dress, and would, as he thought, be glad to purchase at such a price as would repay the "ex-traordinary care and expence that must necessarily be bestowed upon them." He did not print for the many, but only for the few, and he was sanguine enough to believe that the few would pay for the books which he printed a price sufficient to reimburse him for his expense.

Fortunately he obtained an artist for cutting the punches —John Handy—who worked well with him, and yet with Handy to help him, days, months, and years passed before a sin-gle fount was completed. It was not until 1752 that he was able to report progress with a fount of Great Primer.

About this time Baskerville became acquainted with the poet Shenstone, and also met with the London publisher and play-wright, Robert Dodsley, who became a great admirer of Basker-ville's work.

During 1750 and until about the autumn of 1752, Basker-ville quietly proceeded with his type foundry, and in this time the apparatus for printing was being set up in his house. He spent some six or eight hundred pounds upon the types. Of these he said in a letter to Dodsley: "They please me, as I can make nothing more correct. You will observe they strike the eye much more sensibly than the smaller characters. The R wants a few slight touches, and the Y half an hour's correction. We have resolutely set about 13 of the same sized italic capitals, which will not be inferior to the Roman, and I doubt not to complete them in a fortnight." Then he adds, indicating that the time for publishing the Virgil had been already set: "You need be in no pain about our being ready by the time appointed." Baskerville was not to be hurried. He did his work regardless of time and, to an extent, of money. In a later letter, in 1753, he said: "You may depend upon my being ready by your time (Christmas), but if more time could be allowed I should make use of it all in correcting and justifying. So much depends on appearing perfect on first starting."

Of course, the initial labor in preparing type was immense: "He had at first to design his model alphabet letter by letter, so that each letter should bear its due relation to the other letters, on a scale of absolute proportion. The design fixed, the next step was to decide the particular size on which he would begin. . . . Then came the critical manual operation of cutting each letter separately in relief, on steel, to form the punch. . . . Each punch would then have to be hardened and struck into copper to form the matrix, and each matrix would need to be justified and adjusted to the type mould, so as to produce a type not only an xact counterpart of the punch, but absolutely square with every other letter of the fount. . . . The moulds for casting the type . . . would have to be constructed each of a large number of separate pieces of iron and wood, fitted together with the most delicate precision, so that every type would come out uniform in height and body. When matrixes and moulds were ready the operation of casting would ensue. . . . The types would require dressing before they could be used: a delicate operation, consisting in the smoothing away of every chance irregularity left by the casting, without interfering with the mathematical height and squareness of the letter."* Then there were the press and the ink.

Baskerville constructed his own presses. From the beginning, even as early as 1752, he had a press in operation on which he printed his specimens. He wrote to Dodsley: "I have with great pains justified the plate for the Platten & Stone on which it falls, so that they are as perfect planes as it will ever be in my Power to procure, for instance, if you Rest one End of yr plate in the Stone & let the other fall the height of an inch; it falls soft as if you dropped it on feathers or several folds of silk, and when you raise it, you manifestly feel it such (if you'll excuse so unphilosophical a term). Wet the two and either would support the other with a couple of 500 weights added to it, if held perpendicularly. To as perfect a plane I will endeavour to bring the faces of the type if I have time. Nor do I despair of better ink & printing (the character must speak for itself) than has hitherto been seen."

He said in a letter to France, that the presses were exactly of the same construction as other people's, but that he had made them better, especially in the stone and the platen, all of which could be done with a person who gave attention to it; and that in printing he used but one double of finest flannel, other people used two or three double of thick swanskin; and for a description and drawing of his presses he referred to Palmer's "History of Printing," and "The History and Art of Printing," by Luckombe, in which he said there was a print of every part of the press.

* *Reed's Old English Letter Foundries (1882).*

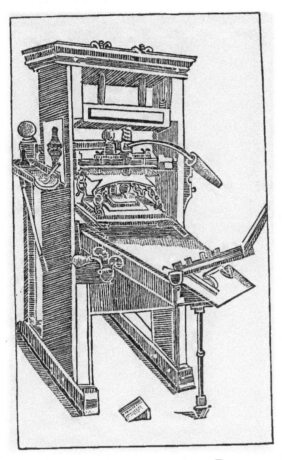

HAND-PRESS SUCH AS WAS USED BY BASKERVILLE

From Luckombe's "History and Art of Printing"

Baskerville appears to have kept a large number "of hot plates of copper ready, between which, as soon as printed (aye, as they were discharged from the tympan) the sheets were inserted; the wet was thus expelled, the ink set, and the trim glossy surface put on all simultaneously."* The peculiar gloss which characterizes the productions of the Baskerville Press is to be found in no other books of the eighteenth century.

Again, as to ink, a black in an impure state had been used by printers for nearly two hundred years, and it was not until Baskerville that any attention was turned to this most essential article. It was reserved for him to discover a superior kind of black for the purpose required. Hansard thinks that to this success may be attributed, in a great measure, the excellence of his printing.

Hansard gives the recipe of Baskerville's ink: "He took of the finest and oldest linseed oil three gallons, this was put into a vessel capable of holding four times the quantity, and boiled with a long-continued fire till it acquired a certain thickness or tenacity, according to the quality of the work it was intended to print, and which was judged of by putting small quantities upon a stone to cool, and then taking it up between the finger and thumb; on opening which, if it drew into a thread an inch long or more, it was considered sufficiently boiled. This mode of boiling can only be acquired by long practice, and requires particular skill and care in the person who superintends the operation, as, for want of this, the most serious consequences . . . have very frequently occurred; the oil thus prepared was suffered to cool, and had then a small quantity of black or amber rosin dissolved in it, after which it was allowed some months to sub-

* *Hansard's Typographia (1825), page 311.*

side; it was then mixed with the fine black, before named, to a proper thickness, and ground for use."*

The lamp-black of commerce is crude and impure, but for two hundred years it satisfied the makers of printing-ink, who made no improvement in their ink. "It was not until the days of the celebrated Baskerville . . . that any attention was turned to this most essential article. . . . It was reserved for him to discover . . . a superior kind of black, . . . and to this success it is said that the superiority of his printing may be attributed."†
Certain it is that it stimulated rivalry in the trade, and a few out of many other attempts to improve were partially successful.

Finally there was the text. Baskerville wrote Dodsley his scheme for obtaining absolutely correct texts of the works he was about to print, as follows: "'Tis this. Two people must be concerned; the one must name every letter, capital, point, reference, accent, etc., that is, in English, must spell every part of every word distinctly, and note down every difference in a book prepared on purpose. Pray oblige me in making the experiment with Mr. James Dodsley in four or five lines of any two editions of an author, and you'll be convinced that it's scarcely possible for the least difference, even of a point, to escape notice. I would recommend and practise the same method in an English author, where most people imagine themselves capable of correcting. Here's another great advantage to me in this humble scheme; at the same time that a proof sheet is correcting, I shall find out the least imperfection in any of the Types that has escaped the founder's notice."

"Meanwhile he had laboured assiduously to complete his promised series of the Roman and Italic faces. At the time of

* *Hansard's Typographia, page 723.*   † *Ibid., page 717.*

the publication of the Virgil, he put forward a quarto sheet
containing specimens of the Great Primer, English, Pica, and
Brevier Roman, and Great Primer and Pica Italic, beautifully
printed. This sheet, which is noted by Renouard, and which is
occasionally found bound up with copies of the Virgil, was very
shortly followed, about the end of the year 1758, by a larger
and more general specimen, consisting entirely of Roman and
Italic letter in eight sizes, viz.: — Double Pica, Great Primer,
English, Pica, Small Pica, Long Primer, Bourgeois, and Brevier.
Of the last two, Roman only is shown. The whole is arranged
in two columns on a broadside sheet, with appropriate titlings,
and forms a beautiful display. Although the only copy we have
seen is printed on a greenish paper, somewhat coarse, the specimen exceeds in elegance and uniformity most, if not all, the
productions of contemporary founders." *

The Virgil was then advertised as follows: "John Baskerville proposes, by the advice and assistance of several learned
men, to print from the Cambridge Edition, corrected with all
possible care, an elegant edition of Virgil. The work will be
printed in quarto, on a very fine writing Royal paper, and with
the above letter. The price of the Volume in sheets will be one
guinea, no part of which will be required till the Book is delivered. It will be put to press as soon as the number of subscribers shall amount to five hundred, whose names will be prefixt
to the work."

Finally, after many delays caused by the desire of Baskerville
to have the book perfect, the Virgil went to press in 1757, after
seven years of careful, patient, persistent work upon it. It was
a surprise to the literary world. It was the first fine book printed

* *Reed's Old English Letter Foundries, page 276.*

in England,—the first of those magnificent editions which, as Macaulay said, "went forth to astonish all the librarians of Europe."* Every part of the volume was in harmony with every other part. There was no disproportion. The book has been well said to be a landmark in the history of typography. In looking at it to-day we wonder how it was done when it was done. It seems as though the Birmingham artist had come before his time.

The list of subscribers printed in the book comprises 513 names, and it is a wonderful list. Scholars and libraries throughout the country are upon it. There is one subscriber from Copenhagen, another from Berlin, and another from the Island of Barbadoes. Dr. Samuel Johnson ordered one copy for his old Oxford College. It is interesting for us to see that the Public Library, Philadelphia, subscribed for a copy, and that "The Library Company at Charles-Town, South Carolina," and " Mr. Isaac Mazyck of Charles-Town in South Carolina," took each a copy, while Benjamin Franklin of Philadelphia subscribed for six. The conservatism of the English bookseller, however, was such that no bookseller subscribed for more than one copy except Dodsley, who was concerned in the making of the book, and took twenty copies.

This first issue of Virgil was in royal quarto, and it was the first book printed on wove paper; that is, as I understand it, on paper laid on flannel or flats, and showing no marks of wires. The critical Harwood pronounced it "the best printed book that the typographical art ever produced."† Dibdin said of it: "I have always considered this beautiful production as one of

* *Macaulay's History of England, volume ii.*
† *Harwood's Classics, page 172.*

the most finished specimens of typography. It was the earliest publication of Baskerville, and all the care and attention of that ingenious printer were devoted to render it unrivalled. He secured his reputation by it, and though it has a few typographical errors, yet it is esteemed by all collectors."

The original issue is distinguished from the subsequent issues of 1757 by the fact that in the original the supplementary names in the list of subscribers numbered four only, while in the re-impressions they numbered twenty-four. In the original the titles on pages 342 and 372 are "Liber Decimus Aeneidos, Liber Undecimus Aeneidos." In the re-impressions they are uniform with the other titles, "Aeneidos, Liber Decimus; Aeneidos, Liber Undecimus." It may also be noticed that on the running-title of page 33, in the original edition, there is a space between the ɪ and ʀ in Vɪʀɢɪʟɪɪ.

Encouraged by the success of his Virgil, Baskerville sought another book of importance to print with his types. Tonson, the London bookseller, had the copyright of Milton, and he finally employed Baskerville to print an edition. This was issued in 1758, and is of signal merit and beauty. Reed says that "as a work of fine printing it equals, if it does not excel, the Virgil." It is worthy of note that the very high gloss on the paper which characterized most of Baskerville's later work is not found either in the Virgil of 1757, or the Milton of 1758. In the list of subscribers for Milton we again find Baskerville's friend, "Benjamin Franklin, Esquire, Philadelphia;" and also "Isaac Norris, Esq., Speaker of the Assembly of Pennsylvania." There are subscribers from Leipsic, Dublin, Berlin, etc., and it is interesting to note that the British bookseller subscribed for 159 copies out of 1113, the total list of subscribers. The first edition of this book was 1500 copies, the second 700 on large paper, and it was reprinted three times in the next two years.

Hansard says: "This work will, in my opinion, bear a comparison, even to its advantage, with those subsequently executed by the first typographer of our age. . . . There is a clearness, a soberness, a softness, and at the same time a spirit, altogether harmonizing in Baskerville's book, that neither of the others, with which I am comparing it, can, I think, fairly claim."* Dibdin says: "These lovely impressions of Baskerville appeared twice in octavo, 1758 and 1760—and once in 4to. 1759. But the octavos have a quarto aspect. I find that a delicious copy bound in the morocco of the day, is priced at £3.10. I know of no *parlour-reading* like that of Milton in one of the editions of Baskerville."†

The folio edition of the Bible, printed at Cambridge under the patronage of the university, was really Baskerville's *magnum opus*. It was the most ambitious of his undertakings, and I think one of the most artistic of his productions, but it was a financial failure. In his proposal for it he said: "The great expence, with which this Work will necessarily be attended, renders it not only imprudent, but absolutely impossible for the Editor to venture on it, without the assistance of a Subscription. And he is encouraged to hope, as he has already received the public approbation of his Labours, that they will continue to favour his ambition, and to enable him to make this one Work as correct, elegant, and perfect as the Importance of it demands. To this end he is determined to spare no Expence, no Care, nor Attention. He builds his Reputation upon the happy Execution

* *Hansard's Typographia, page 311.*
† *Dibdin's Library Companion, page 716.*

of the Undertaking; and begs it may not be imputed to him as a boast, that he hopes to give his country a more correct and beautiful Edition of the Sacred Writings, than has hitherto appeared."

A specimen of this Bible was printed before the end of 1759, and was followed by another specimen dated January 1, 1760. The price was four guineas, in sheets, and the Bible was to be published in three years. Some copies are said to have been printed with a border, but I do not think this was so. In his specimen title-page of 1760 there is a border, and he said it was his ambition to print with such a border, which would appear "more agreeable" to every eye than the coarse red lines commonly used. I think that, finally, Baskerville concluded wisely to print the book with plain margins, and did so. At any rate, so far as is known, no copy was ever printed with a border. The proposal for the subscription stipulated that two guineas should be paid at the time of subscription, but in a subsequent notice in 1761 it was announced that no money would be required until the volume was delivered. In spite of all this, the number of subscribers was only 264, and Baskerville was forced to borrow money to proceed with the book. In 1762 he said the work "is pretty far advanced at Cambridge, which will cost me near £2000, all hired at five per cent." The book was ultimately published in 1763. A few more names came in and a new list of subscribers was printed, but he could not sell half the edition of 1250 copies, and in 1768 he sold the remaining copies, 556, at 36 shillings, to R. Baldwin, a bookseller in London, and even then he had to bring a suit against Baldwin to get his pay. The expense of this edition was doubtless increased by the fact that he was required to print it at Cambridge, and to send his press and workmen there for that purpose. The book itself is one of the most remarkable that Baskerville printed. Dibdin calls it "one of the most beautiful printed books in the world," and says its title-page, "as a piece of printing, is unrivalled, having all the power and brilliancy of copperplate." Cotton, in his "Editions of the Bible," says that the beauty of this book has caused it to find its way into almost every public library where fine and curious books are appreciated; Lowndes also pronounces it one of the most beautiful books ever printed.

In the meantime Baskerville was pushing forward the printing of a Prayer Book, "as perfeſt as I can make it." He said that he would make a size "calculated for people who begin to want speſtacles, but are ashamed to use them in Church." Perhaps this was the reason for the old Oxfordshire Squire refusing to use a Prayer Book which was not a Baskerville.

Baskerville obtained leave from the University of Cambridge to print the Bible in royal folio, and two editions of the Book of Common Prayer. But that learned body appear to have had a stronger inclination for making their privilege conducive to their worldly gain than for earning fame by the encouragement of printing. The university exaſted from Mr. Baskerville £20 per thousand for the oſtavo, and £12.10 per thousand for the duodecimo editions of the Prayer Book; and the Stationers' Company, which had a monopoly of printing, with like liberality took £32 for their permission to print one edition of the Psalms in metre, which was necessary to make the Prayer Book complete.

In a letter in 1757 Baskerville says: "I have pursued the scheme of printing and letter founding for seven years, with the most intense application to the great prejudice of my eyes by the daily use of microscopes, and at the expense of about a thousand pounds, which really makes me short of money."

In 1759 Baskerville was ready to begin the Prayer Book printing at Cambridge. He writes to the Vice-Chancellor of the University, saying he was taking great pains in order to produce a striking title-page and also a specimen of the Bible which he hoped would be ready in about six weeks. He adds that "the importance of the work demands all my attention, not only for my own reputation, but also to convince the world that the University in the honour done me have not entirely misplaced their favours." In this letter he asks the Chancellor if he could make "an interest to a few gentlemen, to whom the work would not be disagreeable, to survey the sheets after my people have corrected them as accurately as they are able, that I might, if possible, be free from every error of the press, for which I would gladly make suitable acknowledgments." I suppose he means payment.

He says he procured "a sealed copy of the Common Prayer with much trouble and expense from the Cathedral of Litchfield, but found it the most inaccurate and ill printed work I ever saw, and returned it with thanks." All Baskerville's Prayer Books are said by Dibdin to have been lovely specimens of presswork. All the copies that remained when he died, together with a considerable number of the Horace of 1762, were purchased of his widow by Mr. Smart, the bookseller at Worcester, for £100. But in a few years after that, not a copy remained unsold.* Smart built a house and called it "Baskerville House."

Dibdin says that "the prayer books of Baskerville are probably more frequently seen within the pews of a church than any

* *Dibdin's Library Companion (1825), page 47.*

other, at least they were so within these dozen years past; they
are of two forms or sizes, royal octavo and crown octavo. The
crown octavo impression, which is the rarer of the two, is executed in a small character, in double columns, upon thin paper,
but of a close and durable texture. I do not remember to have
seen more than one copy of the royal octavo in an *uncut* state,
and of the crown octavo not a single copy, so popular were these
impressions upon a first appearance."

The Addison was issued in 1761, and is a wonderful specimen
of the art of Baskerville. Speaking of this book, Dibdin almost
goes into ecstasies. He says: "He who hath the *Baskerville* edition, 1760, 4to, 4 vols., hath a good and even a glorious performance. It is pleasant (and of course profitable) to turn over
the pages of these lovely tomes, at one's Tusculum [villa], on
a day of oppression from heat, or of confinement from rain —
and if the copy be in goodly calf, full charged, gilt binding—
with marble edges to the leaves — such as Posthumus discards,
but which Atticus dearly doats on — why, so much the better:
so therefore hasten, gallant young Bibliomaniac, with six sov-
ereigns and six shillings to boot, to make yourself *master* of such
a copy."* Dibdin was a true bibliophile.

"Aesop's Fables" were printed for Dodsley, who appears to
have prepared them, perhaps in collaboration with Shenstone.
This edition was ultimately published on February 9, 1761, and
is a very beautiful little production. The book is much marred
by the cuts which Dodsley insisted on putting in. However, it
sold very well, and there was talk of second and third editions.
Speaking of it Warren says: "That book of Baskerville's is the
most charming thing that I have ever touched."

* *Dibdin's Library Companion, page 613.*

Dodsley found Baskerville too expensive. He maintained the warmest interest in Baskerville's work, but found his charges excessive for ordinary purposes of trade. He never allowed him to print anything for him except his "Selected Fables," and he fussed very much about these. He went to Baskerville's house, where he stayed while the last sheets of the "Fables" were passing through the press, and then he printed a London edition in a cheaper form. He complained that he should lose £30 by Baskerville's impression, and that he should not be more than £10 gainer on the whole, taking the Birmingham and London editions together. In 1758 Rev. John Huckell's poem "Avon" was printed by Baskerville and sold by Dodsley, but at the printer's expense and risk. By the persuasion of Shenstone he was induced to permit Baskerville to print another edition of the "Fables" in 1764.* The truth was that Baskerville did not print commercially, while Dodsley published commercially.

The prices charged by Baskerville were very high for the times. He wrote to a man who inquired about prices: "My price for printing your friend's poem is Two Guineas a sheet without pressing, and Two pounds Seven to be pressed as other books which I have printed are pressed." At this price the printing of the poem would have cost twenty guineas. It is needless to say that Baskerville did not print it. It appears that the expense of printing a sheet at a common press was 18 shillings, and the expense at Baskerville's Press about £3.10. This is quite sufficient to explain the disinclination of booksellers to give orders to Baskerville for printing.

The reasons why Baskerville's printing was a financial failure are obvious to us, although they were not to him. In the first

* *Straus, Robert Dodsley, pages 289-292.*

place, he did something new, and that is always a great shock to the British public. He produced type different from any which had been used, and better, but the man whose office was stuffed with Caslon type and Dutch type did not think so. He was not likely to throw away type which printed his books well enough for sale, and buy new type which this gentleman from Birmingham had cut. He said: "Let him cut type, and get a new ink and a new kind of paper and print in a new way. The old type, the old ink, the old paper, and the old way are good enough for me." Baskerville was artistic, the English public was not. In the second place Baskerville's books were so expensively produced that the man who bought one of them as a specimen of Baskerville's work did not wish to buy another. It was the same thing that happens with every printer who does artistic work,—each production of his press exhausts his clientage more or less. And lastly, his books were reprints, and they were brought out at a time when the press was overloaded with productions of very brilliant men. Dr. Johnson's Dictionary, in two volumes, was issued in 1755. Oliver Goldsmith, Pope, Chesterfield, Horace Walpole, Akenside, Colley Cibber, Gray, Dr. Young, Burke, and a host of others were then producing books for the printer.

Baskerville cut a fount of Greek type for the University of Oxford, and cast 300 weight of type at two hundred guineas for the whole. He delivered the types in March, 1761, and was paid the two hundred guineas. His connection with the types ceased here. He did not print the editions of the Greek Testament which appeared at Oxford in 1763. He never visited Oxford, and there is nothing to show that he was ever consulted about the types after they had been delivered. They were said to be "not good ones." William Bowyer, the printer, said that there

were two or three quarto editions on foot, "one at Oxford, far
advanced on new types by Baskerville — by the way, not good
ones." Reed says that "the appearance of the book justified to
some extent the criticism." Regular as the Greek type is, it is stiff
and cramped, and, as Dibdin says, "like no Greek characters I
have ever seen." At another time Dibdin calls the letters large and
distinct. The type was certainly more English than the Greek
types then in use, and was the precursor of numerous types cut
in England during the next century. To the student of to-day
Baskerville's Greek type is far easier to read than any of its
contemporaries. The letters are far from being execrable, as
Mores called them. They are in effect cursive, well formed, and
probably modelled, like those invented by Aldus, upon some
calligraphy of the day. At the time they were condemned as
hybrid, and were used for no other books. The story is very plain.
Oxford wanted a better Greek type than then existed, and employed Baskerville to cut it. He did so, and produced a type
infinitely better than any in existence. Therefore the English
printers, of whom Bowyer was one, rejected it. The old type was
good enough for them. But Baskerville's type held the field and
gave us a finer Greek type than we had before.

Dibdin wrote the following appreciative and discriminating
notice of Baskerville: "With the business of a japanner he united
that of a printer, to which latter he was led from a pure love of
letters, and an ambition to distinguish himself in an art, which he
justly thought superior to every other, and which has perpetu-
ated his name, while the perishable materials of his *japan ware*
have mouldered into dust. It is said he was fastidiously nice in
his attempts at a *perfect letter*, that he did not attain the 'eureka'
till he had expended nearly £800 of his fortune. Finally when

tired of printing, he tried every expedient to dispose of his printing materials, but the caprice or inattention of our booksellers
induced them coldly to reject every overture on the subject. Four
years after the death of Baskerville, in 1775, these types were
purchased by a literary society at Paris, for £3700.*

"Baskerville is said to have been small in stature, and fond
of making the most of his figure by costly dress, and a stately
deportment. He was cheerful and benevolent; at times extremely idle, but of an inventive turn, and prompt to patronize
ingenuity in others; he retained the traces of a handsome man
even during the last twenty-five years of his life; and his civil-
ity to strangers gained him the esteem of all who came to in-
spect his office. Although he printed a sumptuous English Bible
and Greek Testament, he is supposed to have entertained an
aversion to Christianity; and with this view he directed his remains to be interred in a mausoleum in his own grounds. The
typography of Baskerville is eminently beautiful — his letters
are in general of a slender and delicate form, calculated for
an octavo or even quarto, but not sufficiently bold to fill the
space of an imperial folio, as is evident from a view of his great
Bible. He united in a singularly happy manner the elegance
of Plantin with the clearness of the Elzevirs: his 4to and 12mo
Virgil, and small Prayer-book, or 12mo Horace of 1762, suffi-

---

* *Baskerville's work was greatly admired on the Continent, especially
in France. He was paid several very handsome compliments in Pierre
Didot's " Épître sur les Progrès de l'Imprimerie," published in Paris
in 1784; and in the notes to the poem attention is given to his method
of printing and to his glossy paper,—"qui fatigue la vue." To make
such paper, says Didot rather loftily, "is not a secret, and if it ever be-
comes one, will not be worth finding out." This opinion did not, however,
prevent the Didots from attempting to imitate it.*

ciently confirm the truth of this remark. He seems to have been extremely curious in the choice of his paper and ink: the former being in general the fruit of Dutch manufacture, and the latter partaking of a peculiarly soft lustre bordering on purple. In his *Italic letter*, whether capital or small, I think he stands unrivalled; such elegance, freedom, and perfect symmetry being in vain to be looked for among the specimens of Aldus and Colinaeus. In erudition, correctness, or in the multiplicity of valuable publications, he is not to be compared with Bowyer: there are some even who indiscriminately despise all his editions of the classics; but his 4to and 12mo editions of Virgil and Horace defend him from the severity of this censure. Upon the whole, Baskerville was a truly original artist; he struck out a new method of printing in this country, and may be considered as the founder of that luxuriant style of typography which at present so generally prevails; and which seems to have nearly attained perfection in the neatness of Whittingham, the elegance of Bulmer, and the splendor of Bensley."*

The quarto editions by Baskerville of Virgil, Horace, Terence, Lucretius, Juvenal and Persius, and Catullus, etc., Sallust and Florus, in seven volumes, were valued in 1825 at £29.18.6. The Virgil had proof impressions of the plates of Hollar and Ponce; and the Horace contained the engravings of Pine, with a head of the poet from Worlidge's "Gems."

In the specimen of the folio Bible dated in 1760, Baskerville said: "Many gentlemen have wished to see a sett of the Classicks from the Louvre Edition in the Manner, Letter, and Paper, of the Virgil, already published, if they could be purchased at a moderate price; J. Baskerville therefore proposes to

Dibdin's Greek and Latin Classics (1827), vol. ii, pages 555 et seq.

print the same, if he finds proper encouragement; and to proceed with the Poetical Classicks first; and as Juvenal and Persius in one volume is wanting to complete the Cambridge Sett,
he intends publishing that first, at sixteen shillings in sheets."

The first of these, Juvenal and Persius, appeared in 1761,
but the publication of the others was delayed by the printing of
Congreve, Addison, the Book of Common Prayer, and the Bible.
In fact, nothing appears to have been done about the edition
of the Classics until 1770, when there was issued an edition of
Horace, with four plates by Gravelot inserted. I think it is the
finest of all Baskerville's books. It is certainly the most rare,
and is the only volume issued by Baskerville which has plates.
The others, Lucretius, Catullus with Tibullus and Propertius,
and Terence, were issued in 1772, and Sallustius et Florus was
issued in 1773. These, with the Virgil, are the Latin Classics in
quarto printed by Baskerville. They are all wonderful books,
clear and perfect. They were printed in Baskerville's declining
years, but they stamped him as the first printer of his time.

Catullus, Terence, and Horace were also issued in 1772, and
Lucretius in 1773, in 12mo. A 12mo Horace was issued in
1762. It is said to be the most correct, and is thought by some
to be the most beautiful, of all the books that Baskerville
printed. With the exception of Sternhold and Hopkins's Psalms
in metre, and Tate and Brady's Psalms, which were printed in
the same year, this Horace was the first 12mo book that Baskerville printed. The text was chosen by a Scotchman by the name
of John Livie, whom Baskerville employed to edit the book.
He took as a basis for his work a little edition printed at Ham-
burg. Shenstone, who always wanted his finger in every pie,
said of this book: "It is really a beauty, and upon the whole as

good a text as any we have *yet*—but excuse my vanity, who think I could have rendered it better, if they had suffered me to have the *final* determination of it." In another letter he said: "There may be fifty or more preferable readings to what are received in this new Horace, yet you will find a better text there, upon the whole, than in any one edition extant. As to the beauty of type and press-work, it is too obvious to need vindication. The accuracy of the latter almost exceeds what was ever found in any other book."

There was a good deal of fuss between Dodsley, who appears to have sold the book in London, and Baskerville and Shenstone, about plates for this book. Baskerville did not accept any of the designs which were drawn for them, but caused Wale and Grignion to execute a frontispiece and vignette. The book was dedicated to Lord Bute, and the King's drawing-master presented a drawing of the Bute arms, which figure on the dedication page.

Dr. Harwood says that the first edition of Horace, printed in 1762, "is the most beautiful little book, both in regard to type and paper, I ever beheld. It is also the most correct of all Baskerville's editions of the classics; for every sheet was carefully revised by Mr. Livie, who was an elegant scholar." He also adds, "the Quarto edition of 1770 is a very beautiful and extremely scarce work, the rarest of all Baskerville's editions. A good copy, with Gravelot's plates inserted, is valued at £2.2."*

In 1772 the Brothers Molini, who had branches in London and Paris and in Florence, entrusted to Baskerville the task of printing Ariosto. The prospectus that he printed for them in 1772 states: "The Brothers Molini have undertaken to present

* *Harwood's Classics, page 176. See also Dibdin's Classics, volume ii, page 111.*

an Edition which will satisfy the desires of the Public, and correspond with the reputation of this great man. They have used the presses of the famous Baskerville, whose master-pieces of printing all the world knows and admires." The work was issued in 1773, with 47 plates by the most eminent artists of the time. There were 491 subscribers to this book, of whom 230 were in London, 121 in Paris, 8 in Madrid, 14 in Holland, Russia, and Germany, and 118 in Italy. It was a great success.

Dibdin says: "The Baskerville edition of Orlando Furioso with the cuts of Bartolozzi is more exquisite than the splendid edition of Zatta. I never see, or even think of, the lovely edition of Baskerville, of 1773, 8vo, 4 vols., without the most unmixed satisfaction. Paper, printing, drawing, plates—all delight the eye, and gratify the heart, of the thorough-bred bibliomaniacal Virtuoso. This edition has hardly its equal, and certainly not its superior, in any publication with which I am acquainted. Look well to the *proofs* of the plates, which Brunet tells us are sometimes more brilliant in the first two volumes of the octavo, than in those of the quarto, or LARGE PAPER form. But for a drawing-room table, or satinwood book-case, aspire to the quarto: for a companion in green fields, or along quiet lanes, select the octavo." A copy of the quarto impression, bound in green morocco, was sold for £21.* "The engraver Bartolozzi grew weary of the delays of the publisher of these beautiful volumes, who one day in a passion called him an ass, a poltroon, an animal. The artist made no reply; he was working at the moment on the plate of the 43d Chant; without turning from his task, he lightly traced these three words upon the tomb which was engraved upon that plate,—*d'asino, de poltrone, d'animale.*"

Dibdin's Library Companion, page 766.

Did Baskerville make the paper on which his books were printed?

His latest biographers, Straus and Dent, say: "There is no place, so far as is known, where the printer himself acknowledges that the paper used for his book is of his own manufacture." Derrick says: "He manufactures his own paper." He states in several places that he bought paper for the Bible and for other books; that he has it not in his power to furnish paper which is required for the book, etc. But in his introduction to Milton he said that it gave him great satisfaction to find that his edition of Virgil had been so favorably received, and then he adds, "The improvement in the manufacture of the paper, the colour and firmness of the ink were not overlooked." This clearly indicates that he had improved the manufacture of the paper.

He advertised superfine post paper, gilt or plain, glazed or unglazed, of his own manufacture, etc. He was a competitor for the prize at Birmingham in 1772, "for making paper from waste silk." His paper was placed upon the market by Dodsley himself, and went by the name of "Vellum paper." Baskerville is frequently spoken of as having invented that kind of paper. A vellum paper still bears his name. In the "Dictionary of Inventions" there is this reference to Baskerville in the article, "Papier Velin:" "This paper is English, at least we presume it to be, and we believe that Baskerville is the inventor of it; the first edition of his Virgil, which appeared in 1757, was printed in great part on that kind of paper." Augustin Blanché, in his essay upon the "History of Paper and of its Manufacture" (Paris, 1900, page 137), states that at the time of the French Exposition of 1851, the paper manufactured in England was in great part wrapping-paper, but he says: "In 1750, Baskerville invented the method needed to prepare wove paper, on which he printed his famous edition of Virgil."

This view is confirmed by the following from Mores, page 98, note (Nichols): "When Baskerville came to Cambridge, we told him that the exceeding sharpness of his letter, and the glossy whiteness of his paper, both beyond any thing that we had been used to, would certainly offend; and we spoke much in praise of, and shewed him, the paper with an yellow cast, on which H. Stephen's capital editions are printed. This, he told us, he could easily imitate, and accordingly executed some sheets; but they were by no means the thing, the colouring not being uniformly dispersed but clouded or waved like a quire of paper stained with rain."

The paper on which Virgil and Milton were printed has no watermark, and is of a thicker texture, more yellow in color and less glossy in appearance, than the paper on which he subsequently printed. I think he manufactured this paper, but that, finding it more expensive to manufacture it than to buy Dutch paper, he abandoned making paper for printing books, but continued making ornamented post paper for some time. The paper upon which most of Baskerville's books were printed was made in Holland, and it bears four watermarks. These consist of a fleur-de-lis (*cf.* "Edwin and Emma," 1760, and Congreve, 1761), and in another part of the sheet a star and shield with a bar dexter, surmounting the letters L. V. G. This was a Dutch-made paper. Another watermark is found in some sheets of Baskerville's paper. It consists of a crown, a shield bearing a horn, and certain letters of the maker. This is very clearly seen in the end papers of the copy of Addison in the original boards. A slight modification of this watermark is found in a very finely laid paper used only in the second edition of "Aesop's Fables" (1764). The first edition of Aesop was printed on wove paper furnished by Dodsley.

Franklin wrote Baskerville in 1773, acknowledging the receipt of some specimens, and said: "The Specimen I shall distribute by the first ship among the printers of America, and I hope to your advantage. I suppose no orders will come unaccompanied by bills or money, and I would not advise you to give credit, especially as I do not think it will be necessary. The Sheet of Chinese paper, from its size, is a great curiosity. I see the marks of the mould in it. One side is smooth, that, I imagine, is the side that was applied to the smooth side of the kiln on which it was dried. The little ridges on the other side I take to be marks of a brush passed over it to press it against that face in places where it might be kept off by air between, which would otherwise prevent it receiving the smoothness."

Baskerville delivered most of his books in sheets, as was the custom of his day, but one or two were issued in blue paper covers, *i.e.*, "Avon," and "Edwin and Emma;" and others in boards covered with marbled paper. I do not think he issued any books in morocco bindings. They were expensive volumes, and were probably bound up to please themselves by persons who bought them.

All of Baskerville's printing was done in about sixteen years. During this period he printed, as near as can be ascertained, about sixty-seven books. This number is reduced by reprints of the Virgil, the Prayer Books, and some others, so that in reality only between fifty and sixty original books were printed by him. They are not all of equal merit, and I think his reputation as a great printer must ultimately rest upon not more than twelve. These, I take it, will be found to be, Virgil, of 1757; Milton, of 1758; the Book of Common Prayer, of 1760; Folio Bible, of 1763; Aesop's Fables, of 1761; Addison, of 1761; Horace, duodecimo, of 1762; Horace, octavo, of 1770; his editions of the Latin Classics, in 1772, comprising Lucretius, Catullus, Terence, and Sallust and Florus, octavo, in 1774; and Terence and Lucretius, duodecimo; and Orlando Furioso in 1773.

Kippis, in "Biographia Britannica" (1778), page 671, has an article upon Baskerville. He says: "These publications rank the name of Baskerville with those persons who have the most contributed, at least in modern times, to the beauty and improvement of the art of printing. Indeed, it is needless to say to what perfection he has brought this excellent art. The paper, the type, and the whole execution of the works performed by him are the best testimonies of their merit."

Baskerville certainly brought the art of printing to a degree of perfection till then unknown in England. He trusted nothing to the manufacture of others. "He was at once his own manufacturer of ink, presses, chases, moulds for casting, and all the apparatus for printing, and he also made some of the paper upon which he printed his books. The means by which he produced these masterpieces of printing are excluded from the province of printing in these days, by the triple incongruities of *fine* as possible — *quick* as possible — *cheap* as possible," and as has before been said, his trade of japanning book-work was conducted as follows: "He had a constant succession of hot plates of copper ready, between which, as soon as printed . . . the sheets were inserted. The wet was thus expelled, the ink set, and a glossy surface put on all simultaneously."*

Hansard's Typographia, page 311.

Reed says that "However well the method of hot pressing may have answered at the time, the discoloration of his books still preserved in the British Museum and elsewhere, shows that the brilliance thus imparted was most tawdry and ephemeral." This is not true, as is shown by the specimens I have. They are nearly all in perfect condition. Of course some of them are foxed, or spotted, but no more than other books of the time, while the most of them are in absolutely perfect condition.

"Baskerville first introduced into England what is generally termed '*fine printing*,' by producing a type of superior elegance, and an ink which gave additional beauty to the type. The peculiar excellence attached to his types and the celebrity he consequently attained gave a stimulus to the exertions and called forth the emulation of British printers."* Fine work has therefore been progressively improving.

In the "Bibliography of Printing," published in 1880, Baskerville is termed a celebrated printer. It is said his type is "admired for its elegance even at the present day, and books printed by him now bear a very high value. He introduced great improvements in nearly every branch of printing, and produced many masterpieces of typography."†

"Baskerville is the only English printer who, up to his time, had received the stamp of foreign reputation or approbation. He was an artistic printer, for to secure beauty in typography, art must be applied to the paper, and tone of the paper, margin, ink, spacing, size of type, &c. The secret is a finding out an elegant proportion in all, *i.e.*, in a small book the type should not be thick or too black, nay, even in the shape, cutting of a

* *Horne's An Introduction to the Study of Bibliography, vol. i, page 253.*
† *Bibliography of Printing, page 37.*

letter, quality and fitness is evoked. It should harmonise with the mass of letters, and yet be distinct."*

In 1762 Baskerville found that he was carrying his type-founding and printing at the expense of his japanning business; as he wrote to Franklin, "Had I no other dependence than type-founding and printing, I must starve." Apparently he became tired of his typographic work, considering it too expensive and too much unappreciated, and desired to sell it. One of his friends suggested that he apply to the government for aid, the result of which was that he wrote the following letter to Horace Walpole, then a member of Parliament, and an author of high repute:

> To the Honble Horace Walpole, Esq. Member
> of Parliament: in Arlington Street
>
>   London
>
>   this

Sᴿ   *Easy Hill, Birmingham, 2 Nov. 1762*

As the Patron and Encourager of Arts, and particularly of that of Printing, I have taken the Liberty of sending you a Speci-men of mine, begun ten years ago at the age of forty seven, and prosecuted ever since with the utmost Care and Attention, on the strongest Presumption, that if I could fairly excel in this divine Art, it would make my Affairs easy or at least give me bread. But alas! in both I was mistaken. The Book-sellers do not chuse to encourage me, tho I have offered them as low terms as I could possibly live by; nor dare I attempt an old Copy, till a Lawsuit relating to that affair is determined.

The University of Cambridge has given me a Grant to print there 8vo. & 12mo. Common prayer Books; but under such

* *Fitzgerald's The Book Fancier, page 77.*

Shackles as greatly hurt me. I pay them for the former twenty, & for the latter twelve pound ten shillings the thousand, & to the Stationers Company thirty two pound for their permission to print one Edition of the Psalms in Metre to the small prayer book: add to this the great Expence of double and treble Carriage, & the inconvenience of a Printing House an hundred Miles off. All this Summer I have had nothing to print at Home. My folio Bible is pretty far advanced at Cambridge, which will cost me near £2000. all hired at 5 p Cent. If this does not sell, I shall be obliged to sacrifice a small Patrimony which brings me in [£74] a Year to this Business of Printing; which I am heartily tired of & repent I ev[er] attempted. It is surely a particular hardship that I should not get Bread in my own Country (and it is too late to go abroad) after having acquired the Reputation excelling in the most useful Art known to Mankind; while every one who excels as a Player, Fidler, Dancer, &c not only lives in Affluence, but has it [in] their power to save a Fortune.

I have sent a few Specimens (same as the enclosed) to the Courts of Russia and Denmark, and shall endeavour to do the same to most of the Courts of Europe; in hopes of finding in some one of them a purchaser of the whole Scheme, on the Condition of my never attempting another Type. I was saying this to a particular Friend, who reproached me with not giving my own Country the Preference, as it would (he was pleased to say) be a national Reproach to lose it. I told him, nothing but the greatest Necessity would put me upon it; and even then I should resign it with the utmost Reluctance. He observed, the Parliament had given a handsome Premium for a quack Medecine; & he doubted not, if my Affair was properly brought before the House of Commons, but some Regard would be paid to it; I replyed, I durst not presume to petition the House, unless encouraged by some of the Members, who might do me the Honor to promote it, of which I saw not the least hopes or Probability.

Thus Sʳ I have taken the Liberty of laying before You my Affairs, without the least Aggravation; & humbly hope Your Patronage; To whom can I apply for proteƈtion but the Great, who alone have it in their Power to serve me?

I rely on your Candor as a Lover of the Arts; to excuse this Presumption in

Yʳ most obedient

and most humble Servant

JOHN BASKERVILLE

PS. The folding of the Specimens will be taken out by laying them a short time between damped Papers. N B. the Ink, Presses, Chases, Moulds for casting & all the apparatus for printing were made in my own Shops.

This letter is interesting as showing not only the embarrassments under which Baskerville labored, but the relation which existed between the type-founder and printer and the member of Parliament at that time. Baskerville was a British tradesman, and dearly loved anybody that was in power. Nothing came of this letter. I cannot ascertain that Walpole paid any attention to it. Baskerville then went to Paris to endeavor to sell his letter-founding and printing establishment. He asked £8000, which was declined as being too much. Negotiations were again renewed, in 1765, through the medium of Franklin, who was in Paris, and the price was reduced to £6000. But Franklin wrote that the French government was too poor to buy it; that they had not money enough to keep their public buildings in repair, and so nothing came of the attempt to sell during Baskerville's life. Upon his death his widow advertised the business for sale, and stated at the same time that she continued the business of letter-founding in all parts. Apparently she received no offer, and on December 11, 1775, she advertised all the printing material for sale at auction on the third of January, 1776, saying that it consisted of " Four accurate improved Printing Presses; several large Founts of Type, different Sizes; with Cases, Frames, screwed Chases, and every other useful Apparatus in that Branch of Trade." For some reason this auction was postponed until April 1, when a few founts of type were sold. Apparently the printers were afraid of the popular prejudice against Baskerville's type.

It was then suggested by Dr. Harwood, the distinguished bibliographer, that the nation should purchase the types as a nucleus of a national typography, which he wished to see established. Unfortunately his efforts came to nothing, and then Mrs. Baskerville advertised the types for sale again, saying that she would "conform to sell them at the same Prices with other Letter founders." Only one purchaser appears to have embraced this offer, Mr. James Bridgewater, who printed an edition of Hervey's " Meditations" "with a new type cast on purpose by Mrs. Baskerville." Having exhausted all efforts to sell the type in England, Sarah Baskerville, in 1779, sold it for £3700 to a French society, which was founded by Beaumarchais for the purpose of buying the type and printing a complete edition of Voltaire. As, however, nearly half of Voltaire's works were prohibited in France at that time, and frequently editions were burned, and men who bought and read them were sent to prison, it was found necessary to establish the printing-press at Kehl, near Strassburg, in a deserted fort. Toward the end of 1780 proposals appeared and were secretly circulated through France, and two years later proposals in English were distributed openly in England. Finally, after repeated delays from various causes, the edition of 15,000 copies was printed in 1789. Of these only 2000 copies found subscribers, and the entire enterprise was a financial disaster.

Perhaps the greatest compliment paid to the memory of Baskerville was this edition of the works of Voltaire. The Kehl Press was finally broken up about 1810, although before that time some of the type was sent to Paris and sold. This is shown by the fact that certain books printed in Paris between 1790 and 1806 were printed with Baskerville's type, and an advertisement of the sale of Baskerville type, printed with the types themselves in black and red, which is in the possession of the Merrymount Press, Boston, was issued early in the nineteenth century. This begins: "The store-room of the Foundry of Baskerville, which presents to printers a new resource in this art, contains the types hereafter mentioned," and closes as follows: "We will send out a sample of proofs of said types, with their price, while we are completing a Specimen or Book of Proofs of all that the Foundry of Baskerville contains."

Reed also calls attention to four works of Alfieri, all bearing the imprint, *dalla Tipografia di Kehl, co' caratteri di Baskerville,* and dated severally 1786, 1795, 1800, and 1809. These trace the survival of the Baskerville types to a date twenty years later than that at which they are commonly supposed to have perished. "It is to be hoped," says Reed, "that their discovery may in due time reward the patience of those whose ambition it is to recover for their native land these precious relics of the most brilliant of all the English letter-founders." * It is impossible to say precisely what became of the Baskerville founts which had gone to France, but so late as 1891, a book appeared in France professedly printed *en Caractère Baskerville du xviii siècle*. This may be a contemporary French copy of Baskerville's work. The last book printed in England with the Baskerville imprint and with his types was a reprint of Berners's "Treatyse of Fysshinge wyth an Angle," published by Pickering in 1827.

William Martin, who cut the types for the famous Shakespeare Press of Boydell and Nicol, acquired his first knowledge of the art of type-founding at the Baskerville, Birmingham, Foundry. He produced the founts of type from which the works of the Shakespeare Press were printed, and, regarded simply as type-specimens, the productions of the Shakespeare Press justify his reputation as a worthy disciple of his great master, Baskerville. His Roman and Italic types were cut in decided imitation of the famous Birmingham models; although Hansard points out with disapproval that in certain particulars he attempted unwisely to vary the design. "As to the type," he says, "the modern artist, Mr. Martin, has made an effort to cut the ceriphs and hair strokes excessively sharp and fine; the long *ſ* is discarded, and some trifling changes are introduced; but the letter does not stand so true or well in line as Baskerville's, and, as to the Italic, the Birmingham artist will be found to far excel."†

When, on the 25th day of March, 1779, Charles Whittingham was apprenticed to learn "the art and mysteries of print-

* *Reed's Old English Letter Foundries, pages 286, 287.*
† *Ibid., page 332.*

ing, bookbinding and stationery," the "art and mysteries of printing" had very much fallen into decay in England. Only one man, John Baskerville, seemed to have had the ambition, the skill, or the courage to make the business anything better than a plain trade. Even he, with money at his command, after six years of experiment and ten years of production, abandoned his attempt to create an English taste for fine printing. He produced books that astonished people who were sufficiently interested to examine them, and delighted the smaller number who purchased them, but when one went into the manufacture of paper, type, and all the apparatus of printing, it was not enough that he should be called one of the best printers of the world, he needed profit. The fact was that English people did not concern themselves with Baskerville's enterprise in printing because they knew little, and cared less, about fine printing. The young Whittingham, who was learning his trade at Coventry as an apprentice, undoubtedly heard of Baskerville's strange hazard at Birmingham, which was only a few miles away. A tradition survives that he saw some of Baskerville's admirable volumes and conceived an ambition to excel in the same direction. It is probable that Whittingham went from Coventry to Birmingham when he was free of his apprenticeship, and studied at the famous Baskerville Press, which was then in existence. However that may be, he went to London and set up a press in a garret in Dean Street, Fetter Lane, hence the Chiswick Press and the productions of Pickering.

Baskerville considered the title-page to be a part of the book which required the most painstaking care, and he certainly produced a series of title-pages that have never been excelled. It had been the custom to crowd as much information about the

book as possible upon the title-page. On the other hand, Baskerville endeavored to make his title-pages as concise as possible,
and wherever a long title was necessary, as it was in the Prayer
Books, he so chose the type and spaced the lines that there was
no fault to be found. The title-page to his Bible is probably the
most beautiful of them all, although the title-page to the New
Testament is even more simple than the title-page to the book
itself. It is a beautiful page and fine printing, without a super-
fluous line or an irritating decoration. It is a relief to turn from
the crowded and rubricated red-line title-pages of the period to
the restful simplicity of the title-pages of Baskerville.

And yet the master of the art of printing in the twentieth
century wrote of Baskerville's title-pages as follows: "There
was then and there is now a rule obeyed by many printers that
the main display line of a title must always be a full line. If the
letters are too few the type must be widely spaced and one or
more of these lines must fill the measure. No printer observed
this rule more rigidly than Baskerville. Not only in his edition of
Catullus, but in his quarto editions of Virgil, Juvenal, and Persius, the letters of the titles are spread over the page as if they
had been dislocated by explosion. Even in the title-page of his
Book of Common Prayer, for which he laid out more lines of display than could be gracefully put upon the page with a needed
relief of white space, the letters in some lines are wedged widely
apart in a useless attempt to give the lines the desired promi-
nence. It is a handbill, not a title."* He should have reproduced the title-page of the New Testament as an answer to this
harsh criticism.

* *Theodore Low De Vinne's Title-Pages as seen by a Printer (1901),
pages 154, 155.*

In the early days, a printer's type was his own. He made it and used it. He did not sell it. English-cast types did not become a marketable ware for more than a century after printing was introduced into England. As late as 1799, it was the statute law in England that no one should be allowed to possess or use a printing-press or types for printing without giving notice to a justice of the peace and obtaining a certificate, and any justice of the peace might issue a warrant to search any premises and seize any press or printing-types not thus certificated. This remained the law with regard to type-founding until 1869; but happily the law was not enforced, except for a few years after it was passed. Printers received patents and monopolies for printing certain books. The result was great degeneracy in the quality of printing. A privileged printer, sure of his monopoly, had no inducement to execute good work at more cost or pains than was necessary. Old type would do as well as new, and bad type as well as good. The typography of the whole Stuart period is a disgrace to English art.*

Printing in England in the early part of the eighteenth century was in a sorry state. Official broadsides, political pamphlets, works of literature, and even Bibles show a depression and degeneration so marked that one is tempted to believe the art of printing was rapidly becoming lost in a wilderness of what may be termed "Brown sheets and sorry letter." No foundry was contributing anything towards the revival of good printing, with the exception of the Oxford University, and Oxford owed its founts to gifts procured mainly from abroad. Scarcely one good piece of printing was the impression of English type, and even the Scotch printers were rebuked for not stocking their

Reed's Old English Letter Foundries, pages 134, 136.

cases with Dutch type. Tonson, the foremost English printer, is said on one occasion to have lodged in Amsterdam while a founder there was casting him £300 worth of type. James, the only English founder who showed any vitality, owed his success chiefly, if not entirely, to the fact that all his letters were the product of Dutch matrices, and even these, in his hands, were so indifferently cast as to be often as bad as English type. How far this decline was due to the printer or the founder, or how far both were the result of that system of Star Chamber decrees, monopolies, patents, restraints, and privileges which characterized the illiberal days of the Stuarts, it is impossible to say, but the fact is that English typography was in a very bad way.

William Caslon, a gunsmith's apprentice, made the first attempt, about 1720, to found English type, and in 1730 his types were very much used. But the condition of printing was still anything but satisfactory; and although under the influence of Caslon's genius the press was recovering from the reproach under which it lay at the beginning of the century, England was still very far behind her neighbors both in typographical enterprise and achievement. Fine printing was unknown. Once more it was left to an outsider to initiate a new departure; and in 1750 the art of printing found its deliverer in the person of an eccentric Birmingham japanner, Baskerville. To him is due the honor of the first real stride towards a higher level of national typography; an example which became the incentive to that outburst of enthusiasm — that "matrix and puncheon mania," as Dibdin terms it — "which brought forth the series of splendid typographical productions with which the eighteenth century closed and the nineteenth century opened."

The magnificent works which between 1759 and 1772 continued to issue from his press not only confirmed him in his reputation, but raised his name to a unique position among the modern improvers of the art. The paper, the type, and the general execution of his works were such as English readers had not been accustomed to, while the disinterested enthusiasm with which, regardless of profit, he pursued his ideal, fully merited the eulogy of the printer-poet who wrote:

> "O BASKERVILLE! *the anxious wish was thine*
> *Utility with beauty to combine;*
> *To bid the o'erweening thirst of gain subside;*
> *Improvement all thy care and all thy pride;*
> *When* BIRMINGHAM —*for riots and for crimes*
> *Shall meet the long reproach of future times,*
> *Then shall she find amongst our honor'd race,*
> *One name to save her entire disgrace.*"

Straus and Dent say of him: "Baskerville is the English representative of that Renaissance of printing which in a measure helps to distinguish the second half of the eighteenth century. It needs but small bias to place him above that trio of artists —Didot in Paris, Bodoni at Parma, Ibarra at Madrid. Baskerville has been called the English Bodoni, but it would perhaps be fairer to say that Bodoni is the Italian Baskerville. His work cannot compare in bulk with that of the other masters, but we have his reasons for confining his efforts to so small an outlay. The subtle splendor of his work grants it a corner by itself in the world's book-shelf; his own peculiar genius is stamped upon almost every one of his productions. The types themselves were cut upon principles which might well be followed to-day by those who would introduce into their making a geometrical exactitude. Whatever may have been the popular dislike of his work in England at the time, there can be no question that he has had a lasting influence upon all work of the kind after his day. Printers and type-founders alike are indebted to his inventive genius."

Baskerville made his will January 6, 1773, writing it with his own hand. As near as can be ascertained, it disposed of about £12,000. He gave £2000 to discharge a settlement made before marriage to his wife. He also gave her £2000 to be paid out of his book accounts, stock in trade, etc. He gave £500 to his "little favorite," being the granddaughter of his wife, if she lived to be twenty-one years old; if not, the £500 to his wife. He gave £1400 in trust to pay to the children of his nieces, "to become payable on the day of my wife's future marriage, which if she choose I wish her happy equal to her merit, but if she continues a widow the last mentioned legacies are entirely void." He gave £500 to the Protestant Dissenting Charity School in Birmingham towards erecting a commodious building.

Then follows that portion of the will which Dr. Chalmers deemed too indecent to print: "My further will & pleasure is and I Hearby Declare that the Device of Goods & Chattles as Above is upon this Express Condition that my Wife in Concert with my Ex^ors do Cause my Body to be Buried in a Conical Building in my own premises, Heartofore used as a mill which I have lately Raised Higher and painted and in a vault which I have prepared for It. This Doubtless to many may appear a Whim perhaps It is so — But is a whim for many years Resolve'd upon as I have a Hearty Contempt of all Superstition the Farce of a Consecrated Ground the Irish Barbarism of Sure and Certain Hopes &c. I also consider Revelation as It is call'd Exclusive of the Scraps of Morality casually Intermixt with It to be the most Impudent Abuse of Common Sense which Ever was Invented to Befool Mankind. I Expect some srewd Remark will be made on this my Declaration by the Ignorant & Bigotted who cannot Distinguish between Religion & Superstition and are Taught to Believe that morality (by which I understand all the Duties a man ows to God and his fellow Creatures) is not Sufficient to entitle him to Divine favour with professing to believe as they Call It Ceartain Absurd Doctrines & mysteries of which they have no more Conception than a Horse. This Morality Alone I profess to have been my Religion and the [Rule] of my Actions. to which I appeal how far my profession and practice have Been Consistant."

And finally he gave to his executors each "6 Guineas to Buy a Ring which I hope they will Consider as a Keepsake."

Some time before his death, being consulted by friends, who were aware of his opinions, as to how he would be buried, Baskerville said they could "bury him sitting, standing or lying, but he did not think they could bury him flying." *

He was buried in the conical building, previously used as a mill, which he had raised higher and painted, and in a vault which he had prepared, at Easy Hill. The epitaph, written by himself, runs as follows:

* *Secular Review, September 8, 1877.*

STRANGER—
BENEATH THIS CONE IN UNCONSCRATED (*sic*) GROUND
A FRIEND TO THE LIBERTIES OF MANKIND
DIRECTED HIS BODY TO BE INHUM'D
MAY THE EXAMPLE CONTRIBUTE TO EMANCIPATE THY MIND
FROM THE IDLE FEARS OF SUPERSTITION
AND THE WICKED ARTS OF PRIESTHOOD

When Baskerville House was sold to a Mr. Ryland in 1789, the owner did not disturb the body, and it remained for nearly fifty years in comparative peace. During the Birmingham riots of 1791, Baskerville House was stormed, sacked, gutted, and burned. It was not, however, until alterations were made on the property for business purposes that Baskerville's coffin was removed, and taken to a warehouse, where it remained for some time subject to visits from the curious, and even to scientific observations of the condition of the body. Mr. Ryland, ascertaining that a show was made of the remains, insisted that they should be suitably interred, and Mr. Marston, in whose shop the coffin had been placed, applied to the rector of St. Philip's for permission to bury the body there. This was refused on account of Baskerville's atheism, when Mr. Knott, the bookseller, said that he had a vault in Christ's Church, and should consider it an honor to have Baskerville's remains rest there, and they were there placed about 1829. Even here Baskerville's body did not rest permanently, for the necessary extension of Birmingham caused Christ's Church to be demolished, and his remains, which should have been placed in St. Philip's Church by the side of his wife, being again refused interment there by the rector, were placed in one of the catacombs of the Church of England Cemetery at Warstone Lane. And so, finally, after being turned out of the garden at Easy Hill for a canal-wharf, exposed to neglect and ignominy in a plumber's warehouse, interred by stealth in the vaults of Christ's Church, and then again removed by the march of business, Baskerville's bones at last found permanent rest in a quiet cemetery of the Church of England. It is in a spot remote, not easily discoverable, and where few are likely to see the stone, which has been transferred thither from Christ's Church. The inscription upon it reads as follows:

IN THIS CATACOMB RESTS THE REMAINS OF
JOHN BASKERVILLE
THE FAMOUS PRINTER
HE DIED IN 1775, BUT THE PLACE OF HIS BURIAL
WAS UNKNOWN UNTIL
APRIL 12, 1893, WHEN THE OPENING OF THE
UNREGISTERED CATACOMB NO. 521
DISCOVERED A COFFIN, WHICH ON FURTHER
EXAMINATION WAS FOUND TO CONTAIN HIS BODY

What is it that makes the life and work of this middle-aged, vain, and silly Birmingham Englishman interesting to us? Why do we collect his imprints, and why do we talk about him? I think it is because he had the true artistic vision and courage. He conceived the idea of a perfect book, such as had not been printed in England. He did not grow into it. He did not make one book, and then a better one, and then a better one, until at last he achieved the beautiful book. He conceived the book as an artist conceives a statue before he strikes a blow with his chisel into the marble. It was wonderful that he should have done so. He had grown up in a manufacturing and mercantile business, making japan work for sale, and profiting by its sale. Most men never get out of the work and of the ideas of the work which they do until they are fifty years of age. He did. Why was it? I think, as I have said, it was because he had an artistic perception and conceived the thing which he was to do, and adhered to his conception. Everything shows that he wrought in the true artistic spirit: having conceived the thing to be done, he proceeded to do it. All his work was executed upon a hand-press. His printing-office was what we should call a private printing-office in his house. He cut the type; he made the ink and improved the press; he devised the paper; and from start to finish the work was his. Everybody who will do better work than anybody else must have this spirit and conception of the work he proposes, and must adhere to it, or he will not produce perfect work. It is this that makes Baskerville interesting to us, and makes the productions of his little private press treasures in the world of art.

FINIS

BASKERVILLE EDITIONS

IN THE COLLECTION OF J. H. BENTON

[*Numbers refer to Straus and Dent's Bibliography*]

BASKERVILLE EDITIONS

No.	Date	Title

7. 1757. VIRGIL. Opera. Royal 4to. *Plates by Hollar. Map inserted.*

8. 1757. VIRGIL. Opera. Royal 4to. *Extra illustrated.*

15. 1758. MILTON. Paradise Lost. Imperial 8vo.

17. 1758. MILTON. Paradise Regain'd, Imperial 8vo.

20. 1758. [HUCKELL.] Avon. 4to. *Sig. K2 printed 2K.*

22. 1759. MILTON. Paradise Lost. 4to.

23. 1759. MILTON. Paradise Regain'd. 4to.

31. 1760. BOOK OF COMMON PRAYER. [Long lines without borders.] Imperial 8vo. *Finely executed painting on the fore-edge. Price erased.*

32. 1760. BOOK OF COMMON PRAYER. [Long lines with borders.] Imperial 8vo.

38. 1760. [MALLET.] Edwin and Emma. Royal 4to.

40. 1761. BOOK OF COMMON PRAYER. [Double column without borders.] Imperial 8vo.

43. 1761. BOOK OF COMMON PRAYER. [Long lines with borders.] Imperial 8vo.

44. 1761. ÆSOP. Fables. 8vo.

45. 1761. JUVENAL AND PERSIUS. Satyrae. Royal 4to. *Two copies, 2d copy has plates by Hollar inserted.*

46. 1761. CONGREVE. Works. 3 vols. Imperial 8vo.

48. 1761. ADDISON. Works. 4 vols. Royal 4to. *Two copies, one not trimmed and in original boards.*

52. 1762. BOOK OF COMMON PRAYER. [Long lines without borders.] Imperial 8vo.

54. 1762. BOOK OF COMMON PRAYER. [Double column without borders.] 12mo. *Two copies, each with Psalms bound in. See* Nos. *55, 56.*

55. 1762. STERNHOLD AND HOPKINS. Psalms in Metre. 12mo. *Bound at end of larger copy of No. 54.*

56. 1762. TATE AND BRADY. Psalms. 12mo. *Bound at end of smaller copy of No. 54.*

59. 1762. HORACE. Opera. 12mo.

65. 1763. HOLY BIBLE. Cambridge. Imperial folio.

69. 1764. JENNINGS. On Medals. 8vo.

71. 1765. BARCLAY. Apology. Royal 4to.

75. 1766. VIRGIL. Works. By R. Andrews. In English. Imperial 8vo.

78. 1766. VIRGIL. Opera. 8vo. *No frontispiece.*

86. 1770. HORACE. Opera. Royal 4to. *Manuscript errata inserted.*

90. 1772. LUCRETIUS. De rerum natura. Royal 4to.

91. 1772. CATULLUS. . . . Opera. Royal 4to.

92. 1772. CATULLUS. . . . Opera. 12mo.

93. 1772. TERENCE. Comoediae. Royal 4to.

94. 1772. TERENCE. Comoediae. 12mo.

98. 1773. ARIOSTO. Orlando Furioso. 4 vols. Imperial 8vo. *Errata in vol. 4.*

99. 1773. ARIOSTO. Orlando Furioso. 4 vols. Imperial 8vo. *Corrections in text.*

102. 1773. SHAFTESBURY. Characteristics. 3 vols. Imperial 8vo.

104. 1773. LUCRETIUS. De rerum natura. 12mo. *Two copies.*

105. 1773. SALLUSTIUS. . . . Opera. Royal 4to.

109. 1774. SALLUSTIUS. . . . Opera. 12mo.

UNIVERSITY PRESS, OXFORD

113. 1763. NEW TESTAMENT, GREEK. Imperial 8vo. *676 pages.*

SARAH BASKERVILLE

116. 1777. HORACE. Opera. 12mo. *No dedication.*

ROBERT MARTIN

117. 1767. SOMERVILE. The Chase. Imperial 8vo. *This copy reads "chace" on page 43.*

INDEX

INDEX

A

Adam, James, 16.

Addison, Joseph, works of, printed, 34, 46.

Aesop's Fables, edition of, 34, 46.

Akenside, Mark, 36.   [dus.

Aldus Manutius. *See* Manutius, Al-

Alfieri, Vittorio, Conte, works of, printed with Baskerville types, 52.

Anderton, William, type-maker, 19.

Ariosto, edition of, for the Brothers Molini, 41-42.

B

Baldwin, R., London bookseller, buys remainder of edition of Baskerville's Bible, 31.

Banks, Sir Joseph, 16.

Bartolozzi, Francesco, 42.

Baskerville, John, birth and death, 1; settles in Birmingham, teaches writing and practises stone-cutting, 2; builds up great trade in japanned ware, 3, 4, 5, 6, 19; his estate, Easy Hill, 4-6; High Bailiff of Birmingham, 6; his dress, 6, 8, 9; his connection with Mrs. Eaves, marriage, death of son, 7; his private character and habits, 8-9; lack of education, 9, 10; general remarks and quotations on his character and work, 11-19; probable origin of his interest in printing, 19; his statement of his purpose to improve the arts of typefounding and printing, 20-22; his tribute to Caslon, 20; his typemaking, 22-24, 27; construction of presses, 24; his improvement of printing-ink, 25-26; his edition of Virgil, 27-29; of Milton, 29-30; of the Bible, 30-32; of the Book of Common Prayer, 32-34; of Addison, 34; of *Aesop's Fables*, 34-35; of Rev. John Huckell's *Avon*, 35; his prices, 35; reasons of the financial failure of his printing business, 35-36; his Greek type, cut for the University of Oxford, 36-37; notice of, by Dibdin, 37-39; his quarto editions of the classics, 39-41; prints Ariosto, for the Brothers Molini, 41-42; his paper-making, 43-45; does little binding, 45; duration of his printing business, 45; books upon which his fame rests, 45-46; his influence upon the art of printing, 46-47, 57-58; his efforts to sell his business, 48-50; these efforts continued by his widow, 51; sale to a French society, 51; printing-press reëstablished at Kehl, for printing of Voltaire's works, 52; business broken up and type scattered, 52-53; Baskerville's title-pages, 54-55; provisions of his will, 59-60; his tomb and epitaph, 60, 61; successive removals of his remains, 61-62; inscription over last grave, 62; his artistic vision, 62-63; list of his works in collection of J. H. Benton, 67-69.

Baskerville, Sarah, wife of John, 7, 9; advertises her late husband's business for sale, 51; sells to a French society, 51.

Baskerville House. *See* Easy Hill; *also* Smart, Mr.

Beaumarchais, Pierre Augustin Caron de, forms society for printing Voltaire's works with Baskerville's types, 51.

Bedford, Dr. John, quoted, 12.

Bensley, Thomas, 39.

Berners, Juliana, her *Treatyse of Fysshinge wyth an Angle* printed with Baskerville's types, 53.

Bible, edition of, 5, 21, 30-32, 46, 49, 55.

Birmingham, in the early eighteenth century, 1; noted for freedom in religion and in industry, 1, 2.

Blanché, Augustin, quoted, on Baskerville's improvement in paper-making, 43.

Boden, Nicholas, 18.

Bodoni, Giambattista, 58.

Bowyer, William, 13; criticises Baskerville's Greek type, 36-37.

Boydell and Nicol, press of, 53.

Bridgewater, James, buys some of Baskerville's type, 51.

Brunet, Jacques Charles, 42.

Bulmer, William, 39.

Burke, Edmund, 36.

Burton, John Hill, quoted, 14, 15.

Bute, Lord. *See* Stuart, John, 3d Earl of Bute.

C

Cambridge, University of. *See* University of Cambridge.

Carlyle, Alexander, describes visit to Baskerville, 4, 15-16.

Caslon, Samuel, type-founder, 13, 19.

Caslon, William, type-founder, 19, 57; Baskerville's tribute to, 20.

Catullus, edition of, 39, 40, 46, 55.

Chambers, John, quoted, 8, 9, 10.

Chesterfield, 4th Earl of. *See* Stanhope, Philip Dormer, 4th Earl of Chesterfield.

Chiswick Press, 54.

Cibber, Colley, 36.

Classics, Baskerville's quarto editions of, 39-40, 41, 46, 55.

Clive, Robert, Lord Clive, 1.

Colinaeus, Simon de, 38.

Common Prayer, Book of, 5, 21, 32-34, 46, 48, 49.

Cooper, Sir Anthony Ashley, 3d Earl of Shaftesbury, Baskerville's edition of his *Characteristics*, 17.

Cotton, H., on Baskerville's Bible, 32.

Culloden, battle of, 1.

D

Darwin, Dr. Erasmus, 16.

Day, Thomas, 16.

De Vinne, Theodore Low, quoted, on Baskerville's title-pages, 55.

Dent, Robert K. *See* Straus, Ralph, and Robert K. Dent.

Derrick, Samuel, quoted, 5, 43.

Dibdin, Thomas F., quoted, 10, 28, 30, 32, 33-34, 37-39, 42, 57.

Didot, François Ambroise, 58.

Didot, Pierre, quoted, on Baskerville, 38 *n*.

Divine right of kings, collapse of, 1.

Dodsley, James, 26.

Dodsley, Robert, his edition of *Aesop's Fables* printed by Baskerville, 5, 34, 35; Baskerville's acquaintance and correspondence

with, 7, 16, 17, 18, 22, 24, 26, 28; business relations with, 35, 41.
Douglas, tragedy of, 15.

E

Easy Hill, Baskerville's residence, 4-6, 61, 62.
Eaves, Richard, 7.
Eaves, Sarah, wife of Richard. *See* Baskerville, Sarah, wife of John.
Elzevir family, 38.
Enamel, invention of, 3.
English power in the East and in the New World, 1.
Epitaph, 61.

F

Fitzgerald, Percy Hethrington, quoted, 48.
Florus, edition of, 39, 40, 46.
Franklin, Benjamin, 7, 17, 28, 29, 48; letters of, on Baskerville's work, 13-14, 45; undertakes negotiations for Baskerville with French government, 50.
Frederick the Great, 1.

G

Galton, Samuel, 16.
Garbett, Samuel, 15.
German Empire, foundation of, 1.
Gilt buttons, boxes, etc., 3.
Goldsmith, Oliver, 36.
Gravelot, Hubert François Bourguignon, 40, 41.
Gray, Thomas, 36.
Greek type, cut by Baskerville, 36-37.
Grignion, Charles, 41.

H

Handy, John, works for Baskerville, 22.
Hansard, Thomas Curson, gives recipe of Baskerville's ink, 25-26; quoted, on Baskerville's edition of Milton, 30; on his processes of work, 46; his criticism of Martin's types, 53.
Harwood, Edward, quoted, on Baskerville's edition of Virgil, 28; of Horace, 41; suggests that English nation should purchase Baskerville's types, 51.
Herschel, Sir William, 16.
Hervey, James, his *Meditations* printed in Baskerville type, 51.
Hollar, Wenzel, 39.
Home, John, 15.
Horace, edition of, 33, 39, 40, 46; Dr. Harwood's remarks on, 41.
Horne, Thomas Hartwell, quoted, 47.
Hot-pressing, Baskerville's process of, 24-25, 46.
Huckell, Rev. John, his *Avon* printed, 35.
Hudibras, Baskerville's admiration for, 17-18.
Hutton, William, 10; quoted, 6, 8, 11.

I

Ibarra, Joachim, 58.
Ink, printers', 25-26.

J

James, Thomas, type-founder, 57.
Japanned ware, 3, 19.
Johnson, Dr. Samuel, 28, 36.
Juvenal, edition of, 39, 55.

K

Kehl, printing-press at, 52.

Kippis, Andrew, 16, 46.

Knott, Jonathan, 61.

L

Livie, John, edits Horace, for Baskerville, 40, 41.

Lowndes, William Thomas, on Baskerville's Bible, 32.

Luckombe, Philip, 24.

Lucretius, edition of, 39, 40, 46.

Luna Club, Birmingham, 16.

M

Macaulay, Thomas Babington, Baron, quoted, 28.

Manutius, Aldus, 37; Baskerville compared to, 17, 38.

Marston, Mr., of Birmingham, 61.

Martin, William, type-cutter, disciple of Baskerville, 53.

Mazyck, Isaac, 28.

Merrymount Press, 52.

Middle classes, rise of influence of, 1.

Milton, John, edition of his *Paradise Lost*, 10-12, 20, 21, 43, 46.

Minden, battle of, 1.

Molini Brothers, Ariosto printed for, by Baskerville, 41-42.

Montreal, capture, by English, 1.

Mores, Edward Rowe, his abuse of Baskerville, 10, 37; quoted, 12, 44; note upon, 12 *n*.

N

Newton, Thomas, Bp. of Bristol, 21.

Nichols, John, quoted, 12; printer and author, 13.

Noble, Mark, his description of Baskerville, 9; sketch of, 9 *n*.

Norris, Isaac, 29.

O

Orlando Furioso, 42, 46.

Oxford, University of. *See* University of Oxford.

P

Palmer, Samuel, 24.

Paper, Baskerville's manufacture of, 43-45.

Paradise Lost, 10-11, 20.

Paterson, Samuel, 9.

Persius, edition of, 39, 55.

Pickering, William, 54; prints last English book with Baskerville's types, 53.

Pine, John, 39.

Pitt, William, 1st Earl of Chatham, 1.

Plantin, Christophel, 38.

Plassey, battle of, 1.

Ponce, Nicolas, 39.

Pope, Alexander, 36.

Prayer Book. *See* Common Prayer, Book of.

Printing, in England, in seventeenth and early eighteenth centuries, 56, 57.

Propertius, edition of, 40.

Protestant Dissenting Charity School, Birmingham, bequest of Baskerville to, 59.

Psalms, versions of, printed by Baskerville, 32, 40.

R

Reed, Talbot Baines, quoted, on Baskerville's work, 14, 29, 37,

47; on survival of his types, 52, 53; on Martin's types, 53.

Robertson, James Craigie, 15.

Rossbach, battle of, 1.

Ryland, John, 61.

S

Sallust, edition of, 39, 40, 46.

Shaftesbury, 3d Earl of. *See* Cooper, Sir Anthony Ashley.

Shakespeare Press, types used in, 53.

Shenstone, William, 34, 35; Baskerville's acquaintance with, 17, 18, 22; quoted, on Baskerville's edition of Horace, 40-41.

Smart, William, bookseller at Worcester, buys Baskerville prayer books, 33; builds house called "Baskerville House," 33.

Snuff-boxes, 3.

Stanhope, Philip Dormer, 4th Earl of Chesterfield, 36.

Stationers' Company, payment to, for permission to print the Psalms, 32, 48, 49.

Stephen, H., 44.

Sternhold and Hopkins, their version of the Psalms printed by Baskerville, 40.

Straus, Ralph, quotation from his *Robert Dodsley*, showing relations of Dodsley and Baskerville, 16.

Straus, Ralph, and Robert K. Dent, their memoir of Baskerville, quoted, 43, 58.

Stuart, John, 3d Earl of Bute, 41.

T

Tate and Brady, their version of the Psalms printed by Baskerville, 40.

Taylor, John, carries on large business in japanned ware, 3, 4.

Tedder, Henry R., quoted, 16.

Terence, edition of, 39, 40, 46.

Tibullus, edition of, 40.

Title-pages, 54-55.

Tonson, Jacob, London bookseller, employs Baskerville to print an edition of Milton, 21, 28; procures type in Amsterdam, 57.

Type, Baskerville's process of making, 23-24.

U

University of Cambridge, dealings of, with Baskerville, concerning printing of Bible and Prayer Book, 32, 33, 48, 49.

University of Oxford, Baskerville makes Greek type for, 36-37.

V

Viator (pseudonym), quoted, 10-11.

Virgil, editions of, 20, 23, 27-29, 39, 40, 43, 44, 45, 55; subscribers to, 28.

Voltaire, François Marie Arouet de, Baskerville compared to, 9; Baskerville's admiration for, 18; edition of his works in Baskerville's types, 51-52.

W

Wale, Samuel, 41.

Walpole, Horace, 36; letter of Baskerville to, 48-50.

Walpole, Sir Robert, 1st Earl of Orford, 1, 18.

Warren, Mr., quoted, on Baskerville's *Aesop*, 34.

Wedgwood, Josiah, 16.
Wesley, Rev. John, 1.
Whitefield, Rev. George, 1.
Whittingham, Charles, printer, 39, 54.
Withering, Dr. William, 16.

Worlidge, Thomas, 39.

Y

Young, Edward, 36.

Z

Zatta, Antonio, 42.

Lightning Source UK Ltd.
Milton Keynes UK
UKHW041857200920
370228UK00001B/152